Interweavings:

Conversations between

Narrative Therapy

and Christian faith

Interweavings:

Conversations between

Narrative Therapy

and Christian faith.

Richard Cook & Irene Alexander (Editors)

CreateSpace Books
North Charleston, SC

The development, preparation and publication of this work has been undertaken
with great care. However, the publisher and editors are not responsible for any
errors contained herein or for consequences that may ensue from the use of
material or information contained in this work. With regard to case studies, all
names have been changed and care has been taken to change identifying details so
as to protect confidentiality.

**Interweavings: Conversations between Narrative Therapy and Christian
faith/Richard Cook, Irene Alexander, editors.**
Includes bibliographical references
ISBN 1440449740
EAN-13: 9781440449741

Published by CreateSpace Books, North Charleston, SC.
Printed in the USA.

Contents

SECTION TWO: CHRISTIANS PUTTING NARRATIVE IDEAS INTO PRACTICE

Preface

Australia and New Zealand – the down-under countries – are the places where Narrative Therapy first emerged. From there it has spread worldwide alongside the rise of Narrative Psychology, Narrative Research and Narrative Theology to name just a few of the fields of knowledge being influenced by this narrative movement.

But the post-modern philosophy sitting underneath Narrative ideas often presents a challenge to Christians more familiar with modernist ways of knowing that appear to offer a sense of certainty, structure and scientific reliability.

 The Christian practitioners who have contributed to this work have spent years wrestling with Narrative ideas in relation to their Christian faith. Their writing addresses some of the problems and struggles and presents how they, as counsellors, pastors, social workers and academics have responded to the problems and engaged the possibilities, in the aid of transformational work with others.

In **Section One** the interweaving of Narrative ideas and Christian faith is discussed. We (Richard and Irene) trace the key ideas and practices of Narrative Therapy in Chapter 1 providing a backdrop of some prominent postmodern thinkers and pioneers of Narrative Therapy. Our own journeys of interweaving Narrative ideas and Christian faith are traced, we outline the therapeutic practices and refer to seminal writing by which Narrative ideas have been disseminated into the helping community worldwide.

Lex McMillan reports on a research study in Chapter 2. He presents a number of Narrative practitioners who are Christians grappling with the faith challenging questions that Narrative Therapy can pose. It shows how they have made sense of Narrative Therapy from the perspective of their Christian faith, describes six concerns they expressed and how they have reconciled these concerns with their faith. It also summarises some implications for Christians in their relationship with Narrative Therapy.

In Chapter 3 the possibilities of Narrative Therapy to aid the exploration of Christian spiritualities is explored. In this chapter Richard explains how Christian notions of being liberated from the conforming patterns and powers of the social world can be aided by the use of Narrative Therapy. Jesus is described in terms of his own confrontation and resistance of dominant social patterns and powers. His alternatives for spiritual awareness and engagement are also considered. A case study illustrates how these ideas can be useful in the practice of counselling.

Further exploration of ideas of freedom occurs in Chapter 4. Nicola Hoggard Creegan, a theologian and new to the ideas of Narrative Therapy, describes her encounter with these concepts related to her interests in notions of conditioned-ness and freedom. Nicola also unpacks some of the ideas around externalising the voices that impact us negatively, investigating notions of demonic, personal and Godly influences.

Irene engages in a conversation between Narrative ideas and Christian perspectives concerning power in Chapter 5. She shows how one of the major points of conflict between Jesus and the religious leaders was Jesus' challenge of power practices – that he exposed the playacting of the Pharisees who did not practice what they taught and who accepted the places of honour, but whose hearts were far from God. Irene shows how the tendency to power is ever subtle, and how counsellors, pastors and teachers are not immune from using it. This chapter discusses how postmodernism in general, and Narrative Therapy in particular, have critiqued power practices and how Christians can use Narrative to explore our own practices of power and authority.

The relationship between Narrative Theology and Narrative Therapy are discussed by John Meteyard in Chapter 6. This chapter considers how ideas in Narrative Theology might help Christian practitioners to constructively engage with Narrative Therapy. It argues that Narrative Theology does indeed provide one useful frame through which to engage both the possibilities and potential limitations of Narrative Therapy for people-helpers for whom the Christian story fulfils a privileged place.

Irene goes on to explore narrative, suffering and the alternate story in Chapter 7. Core to Christian faith is the theme of life-death-life. This chapter explores the way in which a counsellor can unearth the story of hope by staying with the suffering and finding the values which the suffering inevitably reveals. This chapter shows how counsellors can stay with a story of suffering, and so discover hope from the person's own values implicitly present in their story.

James Arkwright challenges either/or thinking, the binaries in our faith and practice in Chapter 8. Drawing from writers within the soul care genre, he highlights critique of psychological modernism and the pursuit of the perfect self and the perfect life. Discussing the ideas and practices of Johnella Bird, an author influenced by Narrative ideas, he explains how her relational inquiry can facilitate the means by which language can be reconfigured so people can escape being positioned within the binary, in deficit. Several examples of using a relational inquiry are provided and these are briefly compared to Christ's way of relating to people, as portrayed in the Bible.

Section Two is a practical examination of the interweaving of Christian faith and Narrative ideas showing Christians putting Narrative ideas into practice.

In Chapter 9, Donald McMenamin discusses the Self that God knows and compares this with the socially constructed identity. Identity is then defined as the discovery of the God-known Self as a person relates with the social world. Narrative Therapy is presented as an effective means of helping people (in this chapter, teenagers), to make sense of their experience and identify aspects of their God-known Self in order to live this Self more fully and more congruently in the world.

In Chapter 10, Richard reports on a research study on the effects of Narrative ideas on students' identity and practice. This chapter outlines the study, its purpose, methodology and findings and then presents some conclusions as to the contribution learning Narrative makes to Christian students' sense of identity and the understanding and practice of their faith.

Therapists Michelle Youngs and Su Fenwick are interviewed in Chapter 11 on perspectives they have gained as Christians using Narrative Therapy with children. This chapter explores the context of working with children using Narrative ideas which reflects their understanding of Jesus' heart and relational style towards children. It discusses what it means to connect, engage and work intentionally with a child while being acutely aware of their contextual landscape and the way in which power positions both the child and the counsellor. These ideas are illustrated through examples from the practitioners' work.

Irene reports on conversations with pastors John Silver and Jo-Anne Brown in Chapter 12. This chapter explores some of the ways pastors and pastoral counsellors can utilise the concepts and processes of Narrative Therapy in their life and ministry.

Chapter 13 describes the rise of what is being called Emergent Church – that is, new forms of organic, non-institutional faith communities, and the possibilities for the use of Narrative approaches in facilitating such a community. Examples of such a home based community are given to show that Narrative ideas can aid the deconstruction of ideas in circulation within the wider community about self, religion, faith and spirituality, as well as ideas in the Christian sub-culture. These examples show how Narrative ideas can help Christ-followers to know and experience God and Christian community in ways less constrained by traditional ideas and structures, with more of a sense of journey, growth, community and freedom.

As editors, we are grateful to the authors whose chapters have added to this text. In the Postscript, we acknowledge the contribution of these voices on ways to engage fruitfully with others in our various spheres of work and we articulate our hope for an ongoing conversation.

Richard Cook and Irene Alexander

SECTION ONE:
THE INTERWEAVING OF NARRATIVE IDEAS AND
CHRISTIAN FAITH

Chapter 1: The history, ideas and practices of Narrative Therapy.

Richard Cook and Irene Alexander

Introduction

This chapter identifies some of the key ideas underlying the practice of Narrative Therapy and shows how they resonate with our journeys of faith. It describes the inter-weaving of Christian and Narrative ideas that make possible the enrichment of life and faith for those we work with.

Narrative ideas in the contemporary context – Irene's journey

My present work is to co-ordinate courses in counselling and social sciences at graduate and postgraduate level. I am the Dean of Social Sciences at Christian Heritage College where all our courses include Christian worldview ideas and a critique of secular theories as well as Christian perspectives. Both students and staff are constantly challenged to find truth not only through rational and evidence-based learning but also through relationship with God and personal self awareness and reflection of praxis. In learning Narrative Therapy we are seeking to follow Jesus who critiqued the dominant discourses of his day – especially the religious ones, and also to be true to the reality of what brings Life.

As I have encountered Narrative ideas over the last two decades I have been drawn to the innovative practices which draw people into greater freedom, acceptance of the best of who they are, and agency which is both responsible and embracing of Life. All of these I see Jesus articulating also and I am challenged by Narrative ideas to take a fresh look at gospel stories and Christian beliefs. Looking back I find experiences and ideas which led to recognising Narrative ideas as similar to Christian perspectives.

My first counselling training was as a teenager when I took part in a 'Constructive Listening' course at my church. It wasn't difficult for me to learn the basic patterns of reflective listening, the microskills which have become the foundation of counselling training of whichever theoretical framework taught in almost all counselling training in the last thirty years. Narrative Therapy also has, as a basis of training, the skills of paraphrasing, open questions, reflection of feeling which allow counsellors and pastoral carers to provide a respectful space for each counsellee to tell the story of pain or anxiety which prompts them to look for help.

What I did not learn in my first years of counselling training was to find my own voice, to find a sense of myself as a counsellor – that came later. When I first went to university the multilayered nature of my life became more evident. For the first three years I studied psychology – and at that time the major emphasis was Behaviorism with its emphasis on conditioning and shaping behaviour from external input. My Christian beliefs were challenged deeply as I engaged with the implicit doctrines of Behaviorism. I did not at that time have the tools to articulate either my worldview, or the philosophical bases of the disciplines I was learning – an epistemology based in scientific method, and philosophy devoid of God by whatever name or understanding. I also became part of a telephone helpline which offered counselling training, rooted in Rogerian humanistic counselling and the sensitivity groups of the 1960s and early 1970s. Again I did not have the tools to analyse the underlying worldview although I was aware of the attraction of relationships based in 'authenticity and honesty'. Values which Narrative Therapy also espouses but by other names.

For my late teenage years and early twenties my life held these three very different worldviews in juxtaposition – Behavioral psychology,

Humanistic philosophical ideas and practices, and Christian beliefs. I was aware – as Narrative Therapy emphasises – that my life could develop in different directions, that one set of beliefs could become the dominant one and my life would take a different path accordingly. While learning the discipline of scientific method and what I later came to know as masculine Procedural Knowing – the university knowledge skills of rational evidence based argument – I also experienced the acceptance and challenge of honesty about feelings and the self awareness that came with sensitivity training. My faith in God remained steady but my expression and understanding of that was challenged deeply. The charismatic renewal was sweeping through New Zealand and the reality of God's presence was evident in changed lives. These were all converging for me, when as a naïve twenty year old I began to work in a psychiatric hospital as a psychologist, amongst other things, helping diagnose men who were referred for psychiatric assessment after being charged with some crime. In the first months I devoured all of Francis Schaeffer's books, trying to bring together a faith and worldview that was both reasoned and coherent, as well as true to the experiences of the Spirit that I could not deny. There was a conflict for me between my faith, which highly valued the individual, and my hospital experience which seemed to devalue and label – the schizophrenic, the borderline. Years later encountering Narrative Therapy's "the person is not the problem, the problem is the problem", I could identify with the choice to separate the problem from the person, valuing the person as someone made in God's image.

While completing my postgraduate study in counselling rather than psychology one thing became clear - that I did not want to continue with a Behavioristic worldview. I began to look at ways to fulfil my childhood dream of being a missionary. I left the psychiatric hospital grateful for the experience, but convinced that the worldview which led to what I saw even then as pathologising diagnoses and subsequent incarceration, was not the worldview I wanted to choose either. Already I had encountered the multistorying of several worldviews and their practical outcomes in the world of relationships and therapy. I had seen that it was possible to utilise the techniques of Behaviorism while rejecting the mechanistic worldview in which it originated. I had experienced sensitivity training and imbibed the ethos of honesty and self-awareness while also glimpsing and rejecting some of the extremes of practice and promiscuity this led some people into.

In the mid-seventies I joined a go-anywhere-do-anything missionary organisation. All my life I had understood the Christian faith to be counter-cultural. I had seen the split between secular society, ambition, money-making life styles and a spirituality that called each person to a life of faith and responsiveness to God. I was always attracted to alternative ways of being which demonstrated freedom from the overpowering structures of what I saw as self-serving capitalistic endeavours. Growing up as a Christian I understood my faith to be of a minority group, even though New Zealand would have identified itself as a Christian nation.

For the next ten years I lived in various countries, always as part of community, with people who wanted to change the world and were willing to sacrifice everything for that purpose. We shared our money, we lived together, we went without. It was an exciting and idealistic lifestyle and we saw dramatic changes in the lives of the people we worked with. My beliefs were reinforced that people could change dramatically, that one could live outside of the usual structures and mindsets, the usual ways of making money and looking after 'number one', and that we could live according to the ways of Jesus. I would never be able to settle for a life that fitted neatly into the dominant societal discourse, or alternatively 'traditional' Christian church beliefs and lifestyle.

I had always been fascinated with people's differences, and the diversity of motivation and therefore patterns of perceiving the world and each other. During my time in missions I was introduced to a way of helping people understand their own motivation and preferred patterns of behaviour which ever since has stood in stark contrast to both pathological diagnosis, and the labelling of set personality profiles. This analysis of past experiences resulted in a unique description of each individual's preferred way of operating. It was similar to what Narrative approaches would call the alternate story. The process involved the person looking back over their life and recounting points of joy, events where they had experienced a sense of joy, of satisfaction in their activity. The analysis simply clarified the patterns or repetitions of abilities, circumstances and relationships forming an idiosyncratic picture of the person's activities and ways of being. As I worked with people to clarify and articulate these representations, I shared their excitement about their own unique way of being, and the recognition of their preferred ways of operating. When I learned years later of the Narrative process of questioning to find a person's story of, for example, overcoming a problem area of their lives, I recognised the same principles of honouring what is often a hidden story of choices for life. I had learned that people are often almost oblivious to this story until someone intentionally helps them uncover it. I had already seen how articulating this story gives the person more ability to live out the preferred self they have recognised through the process of exploration. I was aware of how important it was to respect the person's own experiences and perceptions, rather than bringing any preconceived ideas. I had already experienced the importance of the listener's curiosity and skill in attending to the hidden or unstated parts of the story. I had also experienced for myself the joy of travelling with someone as they discover a richer sense of themselves from seeing their own story with new eyes. I would often encounter a story from someone's past where they may have done something which they considered, at least in retrospect, to be wrong, and yet the pattern of joy was present – that is, the abilities, circumstances or relationships fitted their preferred ways of being, and so was life-giving for them. I was able to see that asking the question about Right and Wrong in this context was not helpful. As the person could identify their preferred way of being they could choose how they used that understanding.

When I left the missions context I returned to academia to complete my doctorate. My research was in the area of epistemology - how we think about our beliefs and knowledge. I was aware that one of the major divides between Christian perspectives and those of secular society was around the understanding of truth and absolutes. I wanted to understand these differences more. While Narrative is often seen as standing for relativism and a questioning of absolute Truth, my experience is that it helps us question what we have absolutised and relativised, giving us tools to know ourselves and our own knowing more accurately.

To explore these ideas, my research compared the 'ways of knowing' of high school students who were attending either a Christian school or a state school. I had become interested in worldview and one's underlying choices about one's beliefs. I had recognised that my own challenges through my university years were due to my lack of understanding of worldview, and thus my inability to discern the worldview of the teaching I was receiving. I was curious about the beliefs of adolescents, about their own ways of knowing. I was convinced that the 'relativistic' mindset of much of western society would be a major part of the thinking of the students in the state school. I was curious to know whether the students in the Christian schools retained a worldview of absolute Truth. This was the nineties; I now lived in Australia which had declared itself a secular society. Many of the Christian schools which had begun in the city of Brisbane, tended to be very conservative in their belief systems, maintaining a black and white view of truth and morality – in stark contrast to the general trend of Australian culture. I expected to find this reflected in the views of the thirteen-, fourteen-, fifteen-year-olds I surveyed and interviewed. The results of the surveys showed that there were indeed statistically significant differences in the beliefs about truth of those attending Christian schools and those attending state schools. More significant however, was the pattern of their development, and the sophistication of the more articulate students in understanding the complexity of truth. Lyn was a Christian student in a state school. She was intelligent and articulate and even at twelve years old she recognised the need to evaluate what she was learning, and something of the multilayered nature of truth in a complex society:

> ...some stuff in the world you've got to find out for yourself... people can't tell you everything about the world around you, you've got to figure it out for yourself. ...when the teacher or someone might give

you the knowledge you sort of test it out in your head
to see if it's going to work, and you sort of think it
through yourself, until you know it... There's no other
way you can do it, you just have to do it like that
(Brown 1996, p4.1).

Some Christians might perceive Lyn's description as a step into
relativism, and individual ideas of truth, but it is more sophisticated
than that.

To make sense of these students' perceptions it is helpful to
understand some of the previous research in this area. In the 1960s
and 70s William Perry (1981) surveyed Harvard university students.
He described a developmental pattern from dualism (believing in
black and white, right and wrong truth, received from authorities)
through multiplicity (any view is just as good as any other view) to
commitment, involving a recognition that there are ways to evaluate
knowledge and choices to be made in one's acceptance of, and
commitment to, a particular body of knowledge. Belenky, Clinchy,
Goldberger and Tarule (1986) had built on Perry's findings by
interviewing women and asking them about their experiences of
learning, and of knowing. Their book *Women's Ways of Knowing*
became a classic in looking at differences between the way different
people learn and perceive truth, and gave some windows into how
men and women may typically develop differently in these
understandings. Some of their findings became particularly helpful
for me in understanding how Christians tend to perceive truth, and
also eventually in how Narrative approaches aid people in finding
what might be called 'their own truth'.

Both of the research studies cited, and my own research, showed that
many students accept what they are told by authorities. This can be
called received knowledge, because the person simply receives and
accepts what they are told without evaluation. Many people,
especially those with limited education, will maintain this as their
major way of knowing – simply to accept what they are told. Some
Christians would consider this to be a Right way of knowing, that
God has given us people to think for us to tell us the Truth, and we
should accept their authority. This is not my reading of the gospels

and of Paul however. Acts 17:11 is the often quoted example of the Bereans who were of 'noble character' and 'examined the scriptures to see if what Paul said was true.' The obvious implication is that we are to examine what we hear and so know ourselves what we believe and be able to give a 'reason for the hope' that is in us (1 Peter 3: 15).

How we mature from this position of Received Knowing is different for different people. As people experience the complexity of our society, they are challenged to find ways to evaluate 'truth claims'. Some people prefer to hold to Received Knowing. This tends to be the position of fundamentalist churches. The possibilities of moving on from this position however are varied. Some people do simply choose to believe that any truth claim is just as good as any other. This is 'naïve relativism' – naïve in the sense that it does not account for rules of evidence, scientific method, rational argument and so on. Some people take the path that universities tend to teach - Procedural Knowing as Belenky et al call it. This is the more rigorous path of investigation, comparison of knowledge claims, examination of evidence. People who learn these processes well become much less gullible, more sure of their own assessment of ideas, and sometimes more sceptical about religious claims. This can be threatening to faith for some people and so they draw back to a more fundamentalist position. A third way to move away from Received Knowing is simply to focus on intuitive or subjective knowing – I believe this because 'it is my experience', or because 'I know it in my guts'.

While there are advantages for people to hold on to this way of Received Knowing – for, at least they are finding their own voice - it is difficult to reason with this kind of position. It is a similar difficulty as one finds in trying to talk to someone who claims that God has told them something. It may help the person making this claim to hold on to what they believe, but it makes it very difficult for others to share their knowledge or to negotiate ideas. A further way of moving on from Received Knowing is what Belenky et al call Connected Knowing. This is the process we use when we listen to someone else's story and are able to share their knowing, their truth, by hearing their experience from 'the inside' by connecting with them. This is the process counsellors learn to use when they hear another's story without judgment or scepticism. It is not that the listener takes on the other's story as Truth, but she hears it as that person's reality, and allows herself to experience that person's reality 'from the inside'. This listening to each other's stories from the inside, while still holding one's own reality, is a skill – and a gift to the person who may be having their story really heard for the first time. The listener obviously also learns and comes to 'know' something new from this encounter.

There were some significant outcomes for me as a researcher listening to these teenagers explicate their understanding of truth. One of these was my recognition that this generation – both the Christian students and those who were not – lived in a post modern world. I realised that their world was a different culture from the one I had grown up in. Having lived in a mission context I had learned that it is arrogant to expect that I can take my own culture and foist it on those I go to. Rather we were to follow Paul's example in Athens, to understand the culture of those we went to, and to find with them the reality of God in their own context. As a result I saw my own 'Christian culture' with different eyes. I recognised that much of what I had considered 'Christian' was merely cultural. I acknowledged that much of church hierarchical culture, gender roles, power practices, church services, bible exegesis was part of a culture we had inherited, and was not derived from the teachings and example of Jesus at all. In the same way that a missionary, to be effective, must analyse all beliefs and practices, I came to acknowledge that if my generation is to relate our faith to the next generation, we also are called to humbly examine our beliefs and practices.

At the same time as I was exploring epistemological ideas, a number of my friends were still in missionary contexts. It was fascinating to talk with them and find that they were journeying along similar lines as I was. Indeed they were examining their Christian beliefs and recognising that much of what they had held to was really cultural. They told me of evaluating ideas and practices which we had once considered sacred and realising that, in respecting those men and women they were befriending in other cultures, they were changing their own ideas and beliefs. We realised as we talked that the essentials of our faith were very few. A belief in the Divine Other who chooses to relate to humanity, through incarnation in compassion and grace, was the centre of what we held to. This paring away of the inessentials gave a lot more room for hearing other people's experiences and beliefs. This listening to others became a lot like the Connected Listening that Belenky et al described, and a lot less like the enculturation and conversion that early missionaries, (and directive therapists) might have practiced.

When I encountered the ideas of Narrative Therapy there were quite a number of common values and ideas. First the challenging of the dominant cultural ways of being. All my life I had recognised this as part of what Jesus was doing, and as part of my own experience of being outside the dominant culture because of my Christian faith. While some Christians seem to find the Narrative critique of culture disturbing, for me it confirmed what I had always held to – that we are in this world but not of it, we are to question all cultural practices and seek another way of being, another kingdom.

Secondly my unfolding experience as a 'missionary' had taught me to value others' cultures – to look in *their* experience for the presence of the Divine, rather than to impose my ideas of God. Narrative Therapy's honesty about one's own context and beliefs, while respecting and being curious about other people's ideas fitted with my missionary learning. This acknowledgement of implicit culture enabled me to also recognise the postmodern culture of my children's generation which I studied in my doctoral research, and to allow myself to find value – and God's presence - in that culture rather than disregarding it.

Thirdly my learning to look for the story of joy, of the person's subjective inner experience of satisfaction, fitted particularly well with Narrative Therapy's ideas of the alternate story. My learning how to put aside my own preconceived ideas and to value the person's own experience, my recognition of the sometimes long, slow work of questioning and interviewing that this process takes, matched well the Narrative process of seeking the person's own reality of what they valued, and then thickening this alternate story. I had already experienced and deeply questioned what I saw as the often pathologising process of diagnosis and treatment of 'mental illness'. In contrast Rogerian counselling was markedly more respectful of the person, and not surprisingly has become the basis for microskills – the foundation of counselling courses. Narrative Therapy offered a constructive process whereby this respect became an active collaboration between the counsellor and the person consulting with them. My experience of sharing power in this process became a more intentional relationship dynamic through understanding Narrative approaches' transparency around power practices.

Fourth my reading and research around epistemology and concepts of truth opened doors to acknowledging that there are a variety of ways of knowing. This helped me see that believing in a God of truth did not necessitate holding a view of knowledge as only black and white, only received from authorities, only static. I came to see that being a person of faith was much more about relationship with God and less about Right doctrines. Thus when I was confronted with Narrative Therapy's multilayers of knowing, my Christian beliefs were not at odds with it. It became clear to me that as mortals there is much we will never know, and much that we will see 'through a glass darkly' – that faith is not the same as certainty. Rather faith is a trust in God even through the unknowing. *Stages of Faith* by Fowler (1981) clarified for me faith as holding paradox, and I recognised the postmodern emphasis on knowing intuitively as being closer to the way Christians have always had faith, in contrast to the literalist, black and white, 'certain' knowing of modernism.

In describing my own spiritual and intellectual journey and interest in Narrative Therapy, I am not meaning to imply that I agree with everything, nor that my worldview is a postmodern one. I am wanting to give a personalised overview of the trends of the last few decades and show how much of what is seen to be at odds is more cultural than 'Christian versus postmodern'. Having shown my perception of some of the common values and understandings I would like to pinpoint one major area of difference. Having faith in a

God who chooses to be in relationship, to be known, influences every aspect of my worldview and praxis. All new ideas are evaluated in the context of what we already know and believe. For me, and others with a faith in a God who we are coming to know gradually more deeply, all that I learn is brought into the context of that relationship. Sometimes that means my beliefs are modified. Sometimes it means that my acceptance of new ideas is not as thorough-going as someone who does not have a faith. It is a little like being married in contrast to being single. All my choices and learnings are brought into the context of this previous relationship. Sometimes they modify the relationship.

An example of this is my understanding of the self. Narrative Therapy can be understood to say that any 'self' is possible, that we can create the 'self'. For example, Michael White says,

> The form that one would give to one's life when engaging in the creation of self as a work of art would not be the form that one would give to one's life if one was engaged in the 'discovery' of the self (White, 2002, p55).

Christians are much more likely to conceptualise this process as a discovery of the self rather than creation. As a Christian I see each person as being in relationship with God. God knows me inside and out.

There is debate amongst Christians what it means that God knew us before we were born. Some Christians would accept total or partial predestination. But many do not, and I am among these. I agree with what I see as a hope-filled approach to change, which Narrative has. The contrast with Narrative is with the idea of totally authoring my own life. I see that each person co-authors their life with God. We know ourselves in the context of, and because of, our relationships. For the Christian the most important relationship is with God. The discovering of the 'true self' is a process partly looking back at my life, or as Foucault (in White, 2002) says "to collect the already-said, to reassemble that which one could hear or read, and this to an end which is nothing less than the constitution of the self" (p75). It is looking back to times when I have felt most 'at home' with myself and God, and partly in seeking to become what most fits with my values and dreams. If I think that the discovery of the 'true self' is finding a static being, decided on before I was born, to me there is a sense of suffocation or stagnation. If I see this process as a dynamic interchange between God and myself, then that gives freedom and the promise of abundant life. Not all Christians will see this in the same light. Nor will all Narrative therapists. That is the point of this book – this conversation between Narrative Therapy and Christian faith – that we use each other's glasses to give us fresh perspectives and to help us clarify and modify our own views and practices.

Making sense of Narrative ideas while holding on to Christian faith – Richard's journey.

As a teenager, involvement in amateur theatre and then later in professional theatre stimulated my lifelong intrigue as to why people, including me, are the way we are. Developing a character for the stage involves constructing an identity that is convincing. It can only be convincing if we construct memories, experiences and responses to those experiences and the meanings the characters make of them in their purposes and values for living. That in turn prompts the unseen thoughts in between the lines of their speech in the dialogue of the play. Actors are doing this character analysis all the time, sometimes researching similar people in real life in order to construct the building blocks of who we see on stage and in film.

Of course, this is all done using language. Experiences are stored in the actor's mind as stories – just as theorists such as Bruner say we do in real life (Bruner, 1990). But these stories are not just passive recollections of events. They are influential ways of seeing the world, ourselves, others, God, knowledge and reality itself. There are meaning-filled stories about how life is embedded in the remembered stories. When I encountered Narrative Therapy twenty years later, I found it immediately appealing since it has this idea as a basic assumption. As Michael White, one of its founders describes it:

> ...the narrative metaphor proposes that persons live
> their lives by stories – that these stories are shaping
> of life, and that they have real, not imagined effect –
> and that these stories provide the structure of life
> (1991, p28).

Thought-lines going on behind scripted dialogue are also made up of language and this language comes from, as for all of us, the social world. Words convey the meanings prescribed by the social world in which the character lives. This social shaping has always fascinated me. What the character gives value to, what they aim for in life and the amount of choice or free will they can exercise is constrained by the shaping of their world, and their response to it. So the idea of agency – or the power to choose – is in relation or reaction to the social shaping s/he has known (Davies, 1991). The problems that most drama hinges on arise from the character, their so called flaws, the ambitions they long to fulfil and the social and relational dynamics they are seeking to overcome or are subdued by.

These social dynamics are discussed extensively by Jacques Derrida, one of the postmodern philosophers whose ideas have inspired the development of Narrative Therapy. He is famous for showing how influential the social context is on what we can know. Like the real estate slogan, it's our location, location, location – our context and the community we are part of that determines how we interpret words, experiences and possibilities. In his book *Who's afraid of postmodernism: Taking Derrida, Lyotard and Foucault to church,* Smith (2006) helps Christians see how these ideas can enable us to see through the interpretations given to us in contemporary society, to deconstruct it and announce some different good news. It also shows us how important it is to see the meanings of scripture in the context in which they were written – that is, to exegete scripture, rather than just accept an interpretation shaped by modern society's understandings.

As I learned Narrative ideas and practices through my counsellor education in the late 1990's, Romans 12:2 became a guiding verse by which I understood this shaping process – that we are conformed to the pattern of this world and are called to be transformed from this conformity to a different knowing – the goodness of God and God's purposes, ideas and ways of living and being. Again, language is the medium for doing this and our first project is to discern the imperatives in the socially derived language we and others have learned, the messages and prescriptions that shape us.

God's ideas also come to us as language and offer different meanings to shape our living. These alternative stories about the world, truth, our-self, others, life purpose and reality itself can provide another whole set of meanings and perspectives for living and being.

Looking back again to my teenage years, I notice that I had always been intrigued with movies such as *Back to the Future* where changing one choice in the past could produce a different future. I used to wonder what different future I would create if I made a different choice in a particular moment of my life. This meant that when I encountered Narrative ideas, the possibility of creating alternative futures fitted very well for me with Christian ideas.

The Matrix was another of those highly impacting movies. It tells the story of Neo who is unknowingly caught in a make believe virtual world and becomes unplugged from the vast computer simulated reality. Each time I watched it, and there have been many viewings, I saw more ways that our cultural world is a construction, one that the character Morpheus describes as blinding us to the truth that there is more, there is a Reality beyond the construction thought to be so real. I saw becoming 'unplugged' from the dominating social matrix as the Christian purpose – one that Jesus lived and called us to (Cook, 2003).

As an example, growing up with English parents with their cultural background, I came to know the 'reality' of how to be in the world as a set of social expectations passed on using the power of approval and disapproval. Keeping up appearances is a central social message that I discern shapes people in various English social strata. These prescriptions for living are largely uncontested and constrain the free will to exercise choices in line with them or in reaction to them. I later learned the word discourses – meaning the prescriptions and messages embedded in the language of the culture, which we internalise. Discourses tell us what our social group approves of. If we comply we gain a position of esteem and acceptance; if we rebel, we earn the position of unacceptability and usually some form of rejection (Monk, Winslade, Crocket, & Epston, 1997).

As I studied, I realised that these positions created by social discourse are very powerful. They are the way that contemporary Western society conforms us – not in the ways dictators of the past conformed people, but by making us keep up surveillance on ourselves and notice when we're transgressing the acceptable norms (White, 2004). Kuhn (1970) called this a disciplinary matrix– a term I warmed to immediately!

I was struck by another of the philosophers very influential in the development of Narrative ideas - Michel Foucault. I learned how he spoke about those people with more power as able to define what is considered knowledge. So, not only is knowledge a kind of power, but power gives the assumed right to prescribe what is known and true. As Pontius Pilate so poignantly said to Jesus, holding his life in his hands, "What is truth?" (John 18:38). Pilate (on an earthly level), had the power to take life or spare it, so his version of truth was going to prevail and Jesus' version would have to be rejected. If Jesus' version had been allowed to prevail, it would have changed the political world. During my theological training in the late 1980's, I saw how church history is replete with examples of those in power using their position to define what is true and to oppress those who disagree. It is also sprinkled with the stories of people who resisted these prescriptions and announced alternatives. So many were burned, crucified, banished and rebuked. Some like Luther, Francis,

Walden, Hus, Wesley, Teresa of Avila, Catherine of Siena and Florence Nightingale found protection from some quarter and alternative movements were born that offered alternative versions of truth.

From an early age, long conversations with my father about politics gave me an acute awareness of these machinations of power. It alerted me to the ways that people use messages to announce what is 'right' and how this affirmed the position of those who were in line with their ideas and marginalised those who were not. So, being alerted to the arena of national politics, I was fascinated with Foucault's analysis of the way influential people are able to prescribe knowledge and say what is to be true for others. Christians are sometimes disturbed by this as they see the power to define truth threatened. However as Smith (2006) shows, the church has a possibility presented to it in postmodernism to see disciple-making as the co-creation of counter-cultural agents and to be able to discern the claims to truth inherent in a range of media and political presentation.

Perhaps from experiences of school-yard bullying and perhaps from sensitivity to the news reports I viewed, I developed an abhorrence of the way that power is exercised in so many oppressive ways. Suffering, it seemed to me, was usually related to the level of oppression exercised over people who did not fit the dominant ideas I've been talking about in a particular setting. Because of this I was never confused as to why God allowed suffering and oppression – I had never seen it as God's fault. People use power to lord it over others (Matt 20:25-28) in homes, schools, churches, workplaces, communities and countries. Suffering results. Sometimes this is very subtle and sometimes very overt. Naming and opposing whatever form of slavery is being applied (Rom 6-8) has been an ongoing motivation for me. Narrative practices gave me a way to do this – to help people become more aware of the way they are being positioned by dominant messages in their world, to discern the pressures of conformity (Rom 12:1-3) and take up greater agency in alternative constructions of identity and life (Eph 4:21-24).

Again, as I was coming to see it, in this time after the scientific revolution, there is a prevailing view abroad that we can understand all of existence by discovering the natural laws and underlying structures that make us and the world function as it does. This is seen by philosophers such as Lyotard, as a meta-narrative or a grand story, one of the many that are assumed to be true, are legitimating of themselves because they appeal to reason and that tell "an overarching tale about the world" (Smith, 2006, p64). The scientific meta-narrative claims that all existence can be understood in terms of the laws and structures that make it up. This leads to a notion of being able to discover the structures of the self by peeling away the layers like an onion. Behaviour is then seen as resulting from correctly functioning structures making up the identity of the person, and dysfunction as deficit or disorder in these inner structures (Thomas, 2002). Postmodern ideas, such as Lyotard's enable a questioning of this worldview. This helped me see the way history and culture construct the self through social relationships and how the self is not autonomous as many assume, but being produced and reproduced within the social matrix (Burr, 1995).

"The freedom for which we have been set free" (Gal 6:1) has long been an important theme for me. Sitting in a couple of very memorable sermons and hearing casual conversations that convey an idea that Christianity is about changing behaviour have brought grief as I've reflected on the forceful reaction Jesus had to that prescription for living and for spirituality. The anxiety I have witnessed in the counselling room as Christians suffer under the load of behavioural perfectionism has been disturbing. To hear clients say things like, "I'm remembering who I am", and "I couldn't see before how driven I was to perform as a good Christian woman", have shown me the liberating power of an alternative story taking root in their hearts. Seeing God's transformation from what was conformity to social prescriptions is the most fulfilling of all for me. It's like graduation day! It is then I see a person coming to know another reality beyond the social matrix, becoming 'unplugged' and able to live with more fullness and agency in relationship with the goodness of God (2 Cor. 5:17-19).

I value the way that Narrative Therapy sees the counsellor as decentred – not as an expert on this person's life, yet still influential in facilitating this liberating process using respectful curiosity (White, 1997). This kind of curiosity Michel Foucault said, "evokes concern; the care one takes for what exists and could exist…" (1989, p198). I saw this as akin to our call to be the people of God who provide shelter for the wanderer (Is. 58:7), who with genuine curiosity take up a stance respectful of the person (1 Peter 2:17), of humility (Phil 2:3; Is 38:9-20; Col 3:12-15) and who are quietened by the compassion and comfort of God towards us (2 Cor. 1:3).

I became convinced that Narrative ideas and practices offer us a way of seeing the conforming power of the social world. That discourses can inhibit or inspire. That they help us approach the one in need of shelter and see their 'self' not as something they were born as and then just grew up to become, rather as an ongoing creation, wonderfully made (Ps 139) but shaped and conformed by oppressive social discourses, struggling under them sometimes and at other times finding agency in alternative, inspiring and liberating social discourses.

As a lecturer in counselling for eleven years at Bethlehem Tertiary Institute, I have come to view helping people to hunger for the liberation and putting right activity of God (Matt 5:6) as a ministry calling. I see Narrative as helping us fulfil that by the practices it uses based on these philosophical ideas.

One of the Narrative practices I value is seeing the problem as the problem, not the person. It helps us speak about the problem as a dynamic, something separate from the self but which the self is being oppressed by. Externalising this relationship with the problem enables us to map out the social and relational history and the effects of this problem dynamic. We can then listen for sparkling moments (Freedman & Combs, 1996), exceptions, glimmers in the language description where some news of difference or movement is expressed (White, 1986). This is built on Bateson's idea of a double description - listening for the description of the problem's impact on the person, and the relative influence of the person on the problem (Bateson, 1980).

Further, Narrative assists growth by what is termed restorying (White, 2007) where we map out the social and relational history and the effects of these stands against the problem (similar in purpose to Hebrews 10:32). It helps us notice these moments of resistance of and engage in protest at its power (Stacey & Hills, 2001; Gal 5:1).

Narrative work goes on to advance the idea of Remembering. Just as a finger or other bodily member may be re-attached or re-membered, we help people to re-attach forgotten experiences, exceptions to the "story of their life", people who have known and appreciated these different and preferred ways of being. In this way we help build an audience to the alternative story (White, 2007).

So as Narrative is practised with clients, a new story is written. I found one of the earliest and seminal books on Narrative Therapy useful here because it showed the value of also documenting the new developments using Narrative letters, certificates and awards (White & Epston, 1990). These help solidify the alternative identity conclusions and expressions and give them a reality and acknowledgement that people can take with them into life.

Narrative Therapy sits comfortably alongside my sensitivities towards language, identity formation, power, liberation, transformation and new ways of being. I see it as giving ways of identifying the thin traces of subordinate storylines in a person's life and thickening these through rich story development in order to increase agency and decrease vulnerability (White, 2007). The remainder of this book picks up the ideas and practices outlined here. It discusses and demonstrates the interweaving of Christian faith and people-helping practice, showing how Narrative Therapy can facilitate the transformational work of God and God's Spirit as people come to know alternative versions of identity and ways of being in God's community and the world.

References

Bateson, G. (1980). *Mind and nature: A necessary unity.* New York: Bantam Books.

Belenky, M. F., Clinchy, B. M., Goldberger, N. R., & Tarule, J. M. (1986). *Women's ways of knowing: The development of self, voice, and mind.* New York: Basic Books.

Brown, I. S. (1996). *Epistemic development in early adolescence.* Unpublished doctoral thesis. University of Queensland.

Bruner, J. (1990). *Acts of meaning.* Cambridge, MA: Harvard University Press

Burr, V. (1995). *An introduction to social constructionism.* London: Routledge.

Cook, R. (2003). Liberation from conforming social patterns: The possibilities of narrative therapy to aid to exploration of Christian spiritualities. *New Zealand Journal of Counselling,* 24(1), 19-26.

Davies, B. (1991). The concept of agency. *Postmodern Critical Theorising,* 30: 42-53. Foucault, M. (1989). *Foucault live.* New York: Semiotext(e).

Fowler, J. W. (1981). *Stages of faith: The psychology of human development and the quest for meaning.* New York: Harper Collins.

Freedman, J., & Combs, G., (1996). *Narrative therapy: The social construction of preferred realities.* New York: Norton Books

Kuhn, T. (1970). *The structure of the scientific revolution.* Chicago: University of Chicago Press.

Monk, G., Winslade, J., Crocket, K., and Epston, D. (1997). *Narrative therapy in practice: The archaeology of hope.* New York: Norton Books.

Perry, W. G. (1981). Cognitive and ethical growth: The making of meaning. In A. W. Chickering (Ed.). *The Modern American College*. San Francisco: Jossey Bass.

Smith, J. (2006). *Who's afraid of postmodernism: Taking Derrida, Lyotard and Foucault to church*. Grand Rapids, Michigan: Baker Academic

Stacey, K., & Hills, D. (2001). More than protest: Further explorations of alternative metaphors in narrative therapy. *Australia and New Zealand Journal of Family Therapy, 22*(3), 120-128.

Thomas, G. (2002).

White, M. (1986). Negative explanation, restraint, and double description: A template for family therapy. *Family Process, 25,* 169-184.

White, M. (1991). Deconstruction and therapy. *Dulwich Centre Newsletter, 3,* 21-40.

White, M. (1997). *Narratives of therapists' lives*. Adelaide: Dulwich.

White, M. (2002). Alternative identity projects. *The International Journal of Narrative Therapy and Community Work, 3,* 53-56.

White, M. (2004). *Narrative practice and exotic lives*. Adelaide: Dulwich.

White, M. (2007). *Maps of narrative practice*. New York: Norton.

White, M., & Epston, D. (1990). *Narrative means to therapeutic ends*. New York: Norton.

Chapter 2: Stories of encounter: Christianity meets Narrative Therapy

Lex McMillan

About the author

I live near Palmerston North, a provincial university city in Aotearoa-New Zealand. My counselling practice involves relationship and individual therapy, and a training role with Bible College of New Zealand's professional counsellor-education programme. I am married with four daughters and involved in a vibrant Anglican Church.

Introduction

The story of my relationship with Narrative Therapy joins with the story-telling traditions of the sheep-farming community I was born into. A distinctive feature of our family life was the lunchtime conversations where issues as far ranging as philosophy, theology and animal husbandry were talked about, sometimes far into the long afternoons of my early years. As a young man I developed, alongside my love for the land, a deep and abiding interest in human relationships and identity formation. I came to appreciate as a result of these rich early life experiences, that who we find ourselves to be is profoundly influenced by our social contexts.

Now in my middle years, Narrative therapeutic ideas provide me with a satisfying means to consider the multiple ways my life has been storied within its particular social relationships, and to offer others the means to do this too. Narrative ideas have also provided me with the ability to see and consequently make decisions about, the various constructions of power that accompany my relationships with God, myself, others and the earth. When I began to move from a family-cherished role of fifth-generation sheep and cattle farmer to a less well known role of therapist, the warmth and understanding I enjoyed within my family context was edged out by uncertainty and suspicion. I moved from a central place within our family system to the edges; from a place where I could speak and be understood clearly, to a place where I could barely make myself understood. My developing therapist-identity was however supported in unexpected ways that included the discovery that the McMillan family motto adopts the Latin poet, Virgil's words 'Miseris Succurere Disco' - '*I learn to succour the distressed*'. Recognising that I had ancestors who valued these words enough to use them on their clan coat-of-arms greatly supported my ability to re-author my identity from 'a McMillan man who cares for the land', to include 'one who cares for people'.

My growing interest in therapy took us as a family from farming and post-graduate study in counselling philosophies at Otago University, to professional counselling, beginning in England where I studied Christian approaches to counselling. Although I had been aware of Narrative Therapy from my early encounters with counselling methodologies, my training as a Narrative therapist came later. When I did formally study Narrative Therapy I found its relational view of people, in contrast to the structuralist philosophies underlying all of the counselling approaches I had studied to that point, at once exciting *and* threatening to my established structuralist assumptions about people and God. Structuralist therapies view persons as individuals whose problems result from defective internal working such as faulty thinking. For the first ten years of my engagement with therapy I had assumed that knowledge about things is gained through looking *in* and examining detail. Narrative Therapy was now challenging me to look *out* at the relationships between people and things as a source of knowledge. Narrative Therapy was inviting me to recognise and consider ideas that were very new to me.

The late twentieth century emergence of post-structuralist thought has made possible the development of counselling psychologies such as Narrative Therapy. Parallel to, and I suspect linked with this development of post-structuralist philosophy and psychologies, I observe that Christian theology is undergoing a similar evolution in the form of a reawakened interest in the relational nature of God and people. Within this discussion about God as Three Subjectivities, Stanley Grenz (2006) cites twentieth century thinker Richard of Saint

Victor who offered a departure from Augustine's more structuralist approach to explaining God as trinity. Victor looked to persons-in-relationship for the key to understanding the nature of God, and in doing so opened up the way for an anthropology that looks to persons-in-community for the essence of who people are as image bearers of God: *imago Dei*.

When I began to study Narrative Therapy I was propelled into these philosophical and theological discussions about the self, and the associated epistemological questions about how we know what we know about God, truth and one-another. My predominantly structuralist view of people collided with Narrative Therapy's social constructionist philosophy - that the self is a relational achievement. Social Constructionism is a part of the postmodern range of theoretical positions. It challenges the essentialist view that personality resides within a person. Social Constructionism offers a view that personality is socially constructed. John Shotter (1993a & 1993b) puts forward the notion of joint action, moving away from the idea that people do and act as a result of internal psychic structures. In his view a person is a product of social encounters and relationships. Because of this social view of personal identity where change is inevitable, the key issue arises about how a person might be able to make choices about his/her particular identity.

Narrative Therapy's ability to disturb established social constructions of power, and to therefore make choice or agency available, is fundamentally political. Narrative Therapy has the potential to be at once liberating and threatening; liberating for people who have been positioned without voice or agency; threatening for those who benefit from established and taken-for-granted constructions of power. To put this differently Narrative Therapy offers a means to make visible or deconstruct taken-for-granted assumptions about how things ought to be.[1] From a Narrative perspective, these taken for granted

---

[1] This form of deconstruction is theoretically allied to post-structuralist theory. Vivien Burr says of deconstruction that, "it concerns tracing the development of present ways of understanding, of current discourses and representations of people and society, to show how current 'truths' have come to be constituted, how they are maintained and what power relations are carried by them" Burr, V. (1995, p166.)

social assumptions are called discourses. Ian Parker (1992) defines discourse as a system of statements that constructs an object. The discourses that construct Christianity and Christian identity are not immune from Narrative Therapy's deconstructive analyses, and for many Christian people who have been subtly and not so subtly taught not to question their faith, Narrative Therapy can be experienced as a real threat. Richard Middleton and Brian Walsh challenge what amounts to a Christian fear of deconstructing foundational beliefs and meta-narratives. They say, "Deconstruction… potentially clears the ground for the possibility of doing justice to the marginal, for the liberation of those excluded or oppressed under the hegemony of modernity" (1995, p36).

Narrative Therapy's liberative potential is one of the things that resonated with my understanding of the kingdom of God that Jesus inbroke to the world. John Howard Yoder says that the one whose birth Mary announced in her *Magnificat* (Luke 1:46) is an agent of social change, and that Jesus' purpose was not primarily religious but rather social and political. Yoder says, "He comes to break the bondage of his people" (1972, p23). Indeed the early history of Jesus-following bears this out in that the movement had a startling impact on the social conditions of the day. Nicholas Wolterstorff recalls that, "the entrance of the Christian gospel into history worked like a leaven through the Roman world, causing profound changes in the social order" (1983, p4).

A significant part of the struggle I encountered while learning to understand and involve Narrative Therapy in my counselling practice was related to the way it invited me to deconstruct my basic assumptions about the nature of the self and God. Helpfully, Alistair McIntyre observes that the chaos sometimes associated with questioning things previously considered certain is often very disruptive, and can eventually lead to a new search for meaning. He says, "The spiritual chaos occasioned by the postmodern condition does not necessarily lead to the celebration of the death of the self; it may also occasion a new quest for some semblance of meaning" (1984, pp203-4).

As a result of being jostled within this discussion about the relational-self and ultimately the meaning of *imago Dei*, my understandings of who people are have been significantly modified from my earlier uncritically adopted structuralist views of both. Through talking with friends and colleagues during this period of jostling I realised that this experience was not unique to me. My observations were that other people were also encountering disturbance and sometimes significant faith challenge when they began to explore Narrative Therapy.

In order to better understand the relationship between Narrative Therapy and Christian faith I decided in 2002 to explore how followers of Jesus might appropriately and profitably integrate Narrative Therapy into their therapeutic repertoire. To this end my academic supervisor and I designed a qualitative research project in which I interviewed six Christian Narrative therapists with a view to exploring what challenges Narrative Therapy had raised for them, and how they might have resolved these. I used a purposeful sampling method to identify the participants. This involved conversations with members of the academic and counselling communities throughout New Zealand. The aim was to select a small group of people who had studied Narrative Therapy at post-graduate level, were practising Narrative therapists with well-developed understandings of its practices and philosophies, and who identified as Christian. I have called the interviewees quoted in this chapter Jenny, Kevin, Jac, Rob and Ann. Six common challenges emerged in these research conversations.

The most prominent integrative challenge that my interviewees named is the way Narrative Therapy appears to challenge the existence of essential truth, including the existence of God. Writer Robert O Piehl notes this challenge also with this saying, "The central tenet of Narrative Therapy's worldview, the suspect nature of all meta-narratives, represents the greatest challenge to Christian counselors who wish to incorporate Narrative techniques into their repertoire" (2001, p3).

This challenge is closely linked with Narrative Therapy's post-modern, social constructionist philosophy. This post-modern philosophical perspective is that we never really encounter reality and that we are denied the luxury or pretense of claiming naïve, immediate access to the world. It proposes that we can never get outside our knowledge to check its accuracy against 'objective' reality. Our access to objective reality or Truth is always mediated by our own linguistic and conceptual constructions. Encountering these ideas can be experienced as a significant challenge to people who prize certainty in their understandings of God.

Jenny said, "*The idea that truth from a postmodern perspective is a construction of our own reality, and that there is no truth with a capital T, is one of the things that has clashed with some of my fundamentalist ideas about life and Christianity.*" Jac said, "*This is one of the up-front things that hit me, it can sound like the essential-self and truth are being categorised as merely social constructions. This appears to do away with everything, it feels like I am being left with nothing - it is a frightening void.*"

Or, as Kevin put it, "*I think that you would be in danger of losing your belief in God if you allowed yourself to get swayed by these guys about the existence of Truth. I am not primarily a Narrative Therapist, but a man of God who uses these incredibly useful ideas. When John Shotter suggests that I am no more than a locus of discursive influence, I just say, 'Piffle. When are you going to get on with the good stuff?' I do not let them speak to me. Some people are suspicious of Narrative Therapy from the start and reject it. I understand people who say they do not want to have anything to do with Social Constructionism.*"

Jac talked about how he had come to see the need to be careful to make a distinction between the existence of Truth and the accurate knowing of it, saying "*If a Christian person is getting to grips with constructionist ideas, at first sight they seem to be so incompatible. But as they begin to explore it in more depth, and begin to explore possibilities, they might begin to see that there are ways to hold onto at least the <u>existence</u> of God and Truth. Some might find they can be a bit more negotiable about the knowing of God and Truth, the epistemology side, and the place of discourse* *in that. … This raises the question that I believe is one of the primary ones in this debate – does it really matter or not whether we have an essentialist view of personhood, God, or truth? In a sense the more important question is an epistemological one – how we know what we know? What social constructionism and in turn Narrative Therapy is questioning is how we know things and our way of making meaning of things."* Cameron Lee writing in Christianity Today said, "Christians who believe in absolute-truth must be clear about what that means. Postmodern writers have shown how fallible human language and truth-claims can be, and rightly so" (2001, p3).

In the face of the disorientation that I experienced I found it helpful to follow Middleton and Walsh's recommendation to "immerse ourselves in the Bible as the non-negotiable, canonical foundation of our faith" (1995, p174). This provided me with a clear place to stand and from where to reference what I was encountering.

The second integrative challenge that emerged in conversation with the interviewees was the social constructionist denial that people have a structural or essential-self. Kevin said, *"At the time of my training, my colleagues and I were struggling with the very taken-for-granted and hegemonic idea that 'I am who I am'; that at some place or part of me I am someone, and that as a someone I exist quite separately from how we might choose to talk about that something. That it is a fixed stable thing and of course social constructionist ideas challenge that."*

Jac said, *"For a long time I have not found anything very satisfying about the self from a Christian perspective. A lot of what I did find was basically just humanist discourse taken over and dressed as Christian. It was either Jungian or it was Rogerian. Whatever I found had very little that has stood out as distinctly Christian. This has always happened, down through the years it was neo-Platonism and then Rationalism in the Enlightenment era and so I am not sure we can escape that. I think what troubled me about it was that it is so individualistic and people were trying to come up with a view of the self without any relationship factor. It was kind of just the individual self, and this never really made any sense to me. It seemed somewhat idolatrous really. So then to discover, in Constructionism, an inherently relational idea of self-hood has been really positive. There is challenge here, but to me there are also exciting and positive aspects to what Narrative Therapy brings to this. The relationship responsibility ideas, that Kenneth Gergen in particular brings, seem a whole lot more Biblical than some of the things that we seem to have desperately tried to integrate with Christianity in the twentieth century. I think the Social Constructionists are calling us, or rather they call me, to re-examine things and it confirms what I have always felt - and this is the relational emphasis that we find in Christian scriptures."*

Several of the interviewees described how they had developed the ability to cherish that people have both an essential self *and* the new idea that people are also spoken into being through language. Kevin developed the idea of being spoken into being in language, speculating that this might be a part of how God forms people in relationship. Kevin said, *"Social Constructionists talk about 'being spoken into being'. Genesis 1:3 says, 'And God said, "Let there be light," and there was light.' And the Gospel of John begins, 'The Word was with God and the Word was God. What I am wondering is whether the constructive effect of language, right there within what we call thought, could partially be constructive conversation between God and a person."* Rowan Williams appears to be saying something similar. He says "Augustine's *Confessions* is a work permeated on practically every page by the acknowledgement that true knowledge of the self is inseparable from true knowledge of God" (1992, p220).

As I grappled with this issue, I came to adopt a *both-and* approach; that people are both structural and relational. I now recognise the view that the self is a stable structure has been dominant throughout the Western enlightenment period of history, and that this dominance has subordinated relational views of the self. I am supported in this view by Biblical anthropologist James Houston's proposal that the self is at least in part a relational achievement, and additionally proposes that "knowledge of one-self arising in *relationship*, stands in contrast to the secular self-concern as a form of *self-achievable* self-knowledge" (2000, p 313). I have found that I can embrace much of Narrative Therapy now that I have been able to develop a comprehensive Biblical view of persons.

The third integrative challenge that emerged in my interviewee conversations was the concern that deconstructive questioning might dismantle a person's faith in God. When used within the context of Narrative Therapy the practice of deconstructing taken-for-granted ideas and beliefs is central to assisting a person to recognise the social influences that have given rise to his/her identity, and to choosing the basis upon which to develop preferred identity stories. Vivien Burr says of deconstruction that, "it concerns tracing the development of present ways of understanding, of current discourses and representations of people and society, to show how current 'truths' have come to be constituted, how they are maintained and what power relations are carried by them" (1995, p166). One of the main concerns that deconstruction presents Christians with is what to deconstruct and what not to.

Rob said, *"Potentially it may mean that someone might deconstruct their faith out of existence. If a person's faith has been a compliance with some dominant stories and has not been a 'making sense of their own experience of spirituality', then deconstructing may reveal they may not have anything else to make sense of. Theoretically people may end up being without a faith."* I think it is very reasonable to think that non-selective deconstruction can be potentially damaging to faith. Wisdom is needed then in discerning what to deconstruct and what not to.

Middleton and Walsh name two particular concerns with non-selective deconstruction. First, they observe that with liberation comes disorientation, saying, "for all its good intentions, deconstructive therapy can endanger the patient: it can precipitate the loss of a safe world and can expose one to terror … deconstruction confronts us with the claim that all order is arbitrary, imposed on the world by human beings" (1995, p. 36-37). Their second concern is that through deconstruction we can become vulnerable in the stark awareness of our part in the social construction of reality, and in this we come to realize "our complicity in violence …and our complicity in evil" (1995, p. 36-37).

Archibald Hart however suggests that thoughtful questioning of the basic tenants of faith can be useful saying, "It is important that doubts about truth not be judged or discounted offhand, as some Christians tend to do. Doubting of any sort is seen as a sign that one's faith is weak. But is it? It may just mean that the person doubting is a little more honest" (2001, p. 46). I suggest then that some of the doubting that Narrative Therapy surfaces might be seen as evidence of a person's commitment to Truth; a challenging and questioning because s/he wants to know that what they are calling truth is a clear as possible reflection that language can offer of the real thing. In this sense although deconstruction is a potent tool, it has the potential to assist a person to refine faith.

Rob offered a helpful example of where deconstruction can be useful saying, *"I see Narrative Therapy as a powerful tool for inviting people to deconstruct the dominant storying that has oppressed their view and trained them to explain their experience in certain ways, and therefore positioned themselves as inadequate in certain ways. It may enable them to re-story their experience."* Writer Brian McLaren echoes Rob's observation saying that, "Jesus represented good-news in the face of ruling powers, as a liberating revolutionary leader who deconstructed oppressive authority, freeing people from the dehumanizing and oppression that come from all 'the powers that be' in our world including religious powers" (2004, p. 90-91).

Kevin spoke of the term 'schizophrenia' to illustrate deconstructive questioning's ability to support the removal of oppressive versions of identity. Kevin said, *"The nice thing about Social Constructionism is that we can stand back from a label like 'schizophrenic' and look at the effect of that particular description, and not be sucked into the notion that it is necessarily true. We can recognise that it is just one way of describing what is going on here, and that there are others. This is its beauty - that we can deconstruct the positions that language places us in, and thereby makes available some possibility of making choices about which descriptions we apply to ourselves."* Selective deconstruction reminds us to recognise that unity is always purchased with violence, and as Middleton and Walsh say, "we enquire about what (and who) has been left out, silenced or suppressed in all constructions that aspire toward a *total* accounting of reality." Deconstruction in other words, potentially clears the ground for the possibility of doing justice to the marginal and for the liberation of those excluded or oppressed. It also needs to be used with care not to question too much too soon.

Jenny spoke about how she supported herself as she was invited by Narrative Therapy to deconstruct some of her assumptions about her life. She said, *"I think the key is to have people around to help guide you through the process. I had a wonderful supervisor when I started as a therapist, with whom I talked a lot of this stuff through. It was really good to have people who were not going to be thrown by my hard questions."…"It was having someone who did not position themselves in the Christian belief system that actually added to my personal journey. My supervisor posed the questions that no one else actually asked me, she asked questions without any expectation of the boxed answers, and that was really good."*

The fourth integrative challenge to emerge was that Narrative Therapy appears to promote relativism. One of the common misconceptions that I encounter, when people hear that Narrative Therapy is related to post-modernism, is that it is about relativism. Ann articulated this misconception saying, *"I think when I first encountered Narrative Therapy that I was concerned by the idea that postmodernity was in some way connected with it, and the only thing people seemed to associate with postmodernity was that 'anything goes'. That is the way many people would describe it, anything goes - there are no absolutes. So how can you believe in a God who has absolutes from a framework where there are no absolutes? That is where I would have been coming from before I learned to see it differently."*

It is important to recognise that postmodernism and therefore Narrative Therapy is not necessarily questioning the existence of things, such as essential truth and the values that flow from this. It does however claim that because the meaning we make about things is always constructed in language, guided by discourse, our meanings are never accurate reflections of the things being talked about. Jac put it like this, *"it is an epistemological issue, how we know what we know. It is not so much about saying if I think the earth is round and you think it is flat that is ok for me. It is about the discourses that are available for us at any one particular time and how we are constructing meaning from those. We are allowed to say to ourselves at least that some ways of constructing meaning are more useful than others. We are allowed to make comparisons, but it begs the question for what or in what way, and then that comes back to what we want to produce with our lives." "Then there is a tolerance or acceptance that people have differing ways of making meaning, but I do not think it is a live and let live thing, it is about having a project and connecting collaboratively with others who have similar projects."*

To confuse Narrative Therapy with relativism is to overlook its gift which is to make visible the assumptions that have guided our meaning making about things, to enquire what has been overlooked and missed out in choosing one account of the truth, and to therefore provide choice. It is about how we know what we know about things, it is not about whether the things themselves exist or not.

The fifth integrative challenge to emerge from my research conversations relates to the assumption that God has one right path for people to follow in their life. In the light of this assumption the Narrative therapeutic goal of developing personal agency, or choice, may be interpreted as encouraging independence and so undermining of the authority of God in a person's life. If this is a part of how a person's faith is made up then that person might ask why the therapist would be working to develop personal agency because what matters is what God wants. Therefore a person whose faith stories have been built around discourses of God having one right path may well experience threat and fear if a therapist were to invite her to choose how she would like her life to develop.

This integrative challenge illustrates well Narrative Therapy's ability to make visible the discourses that underlie a person's understanding about things, in this case Christian faith. Once Kevin and Jac were able to independently identify the discourse about God only having one right path, they were able to critique it against their Biblical understandings and subsequently replace it with alternative discourses about the nature of Jesus' project in the world. Kevin said, *"The idea that a person is discursively positioned in ways that limit their agency seems to me to be so counter to Christian ideas. Narrative Therapy's ability to liberate people from the grip of discourses that oppress people resonated for me with the way I understand God to work with me. I find God invites me to take charge of my life, and that God speaks to me in ways that really draws me out from myself. I think Christianity is a really agentic faith."*

Jac said, *"I am aware of the danger of just recasting my biblical interpretation in a new constructionist mould as people have done in the past with other philosophical ideas. But I do genuinely believe that Jesus is inviting people toward a greater freedom, away from the things that oppress them and toward a greater measure of freedom. I see Jesus working deconstructively to bring to light the thinking and practices that are underlying the oppression."*

I have been struck with the strength of the recurring theme of liberation that emerges as we explore Narrative Therapy in the light of Jesus' project in the world. Ann said, *"I think that as Narrative therapists, one of the things that we offer to our clients is freedom to be pilgrims in their own lives, to investigate who they are, who they want to be and who God is. It broadens it rather than being a very thin description and it is not good or bad, but just is. It is like something that has a lot of colour; some are dull and difficult things and others are vibrant. Together it makes something that is a lot richer than before. I believe God would rather that we are concerned with having an impact, or spiritual presence, however insignificant in the world, rather than staying safe and seemingly powerful within the confines of the church. I see Jesus as a revolutionary; he did not move with the status quo and we have a church that is trying to keep itself safe."*

The sixth and final integrative challenge identified is Narrative Therapy's ability to challenge established structures of power within the organised religion of Christianity. For some this can be very threatening. Philip Yancey says of the Christian gospel that it is not at all what people would have come up with on our own. "I for one," he says, "would expect to have to clean up my act before even applying for an audience with a Holy God. But Jesus told of God ignoring a fancy religious teacher and turning instead to an ordinary sinner who pleads, 'God have mercy.' Throughout the Bible, in fact, God shows a marked preference for the 'real' people over 'good' people" (1997, p. 54).

In spite of this preference of God's for people to be real, Christianity has managed to interpret people's experiences of God in set and prescribed ways, and as a result people are surrounded by much reduced sets of meanings and implications in their lives. Narrative Therapy is very powerful in deconstructing these beliefs based on narrow sets of meanings, and exposing whether there are other places where people can stand and other ways that people can explain, and make sense of, and live out their faith in God.

Rob said, "I think that this is why some Christians will act against Narrative ideas, because they can see that let loose it could actually dismantle organised Christianity. But I am ok with that because I do not think that would happen in a hurry. Also, because out of that could come some very exciting possibilities, like the rediscovering of some old things that have been part of Christian stories, but that have been crowded out. This is a struggle for Christianity. For someone who comes and hears about Narrative Therapy, and the position they have adopted is 'I am a good Christian who meets these dictates of organised Christianity,' then Narrative Therapy does not even fit with that, because you cannot even mesh it with that story."

Yes Narrative Therapy is exceptionally good at deconstructing and disturbing versions of Christianity that keep people constrained by minute law-keeping, and in the light of Rob's belief that, "Jesus wants to deconstruct and reconstruct the story of what it means to be God's people in relationship," it is also a life-giving gift.

I have come to see that the integrative challenges that arise when Christian faith begins to relate to Narrative Therapy are mostly to do with the organised religion's aversion to challenge. While I am extremely grateful that Jesus represents a God who longs for all of creation to re-experience grace and freedom, I am saddened by the recognition that significant parts of the way the Christian church have forgotten the centrality of relationship within the gospel. Peter Holmes (2005) helpfully notes that if our image of God has been primarily formed in relation to Greek philosophical structures of either/or dualistically, then we will be hindered in our understanding and experience of both a personal God and our own relational personhood.

The concerns I had when I first encountered Narrative Therapy have largely dissolved as it has assisted me to recognise as Archibald Hart says that, "the insistence that we construct our world through community is not too far from what the gospel teaches" (2001, p. 46). Because Narrative Therapy assists us to be intentional about *how* we construct our lives in relationship, I have come to believe that it contains gifts that need to be taken very seriously because they are able to assist the Christian church to live out of a Trinitarian understanding, not built on Greek categories and separation, but rather holism.

References

Burr, V. (1995). *An introduction to social constructionism*. London: Routledge.

Derrida, J. (1978). Violence and metaphysics: An essay on the thought of Emmanuel Levinas. In Alan Bass (Trans.), *Writing and difference.* Chicago: University of Chicago Press.

Evans, C. S. (2006). *Kierkegaard on faith and the self.* Waco, Texas: Baylor University Press.

Gergen, K. J. (1991). *The saturated self: Dilemmas of identity in contemporary life.* New York: Basic Books.

Grenz, S. (2006). The social God and the relational self. In R. Lints, H. Horton & M. Talbot, (Eds.), *Personal identity in theological perspective.* Grand Rapids: Eerdmans.

Grenz, S.J. (2001). *The social God and the relational self: A trinitarian theology of Imago Dei.* Louisville: Westminster John Knox Press.

Hart, A. (2001). Counseling the Postmodern Mind. *Christian Counselling Today, 9*(3).

Holmes, P. R. (2005). *Becoming more human: Exploring the interface of spirituality, discipleship and therapeutic faith community*. Milton Keynes: Paternoster Press.

Houston, J. M. (2000). The double knowledge as the way of wisdom. In J.I. Packer & Sven K. Soderlund (Eds.), *The way of wisdom: Essays in honor of Bruce K. Waltke*. Grand Rapids, MI: Zondervan Publishing House,   pp. 309-313.

Kenneson, P. (1995). *There's no such thing as objective truth, and it's a good thing too*. In T. Phillips, & D. Okholm (Eds.), *Christian apologetics in the postmodern world*. Downers Grove: IVP.

Lee, C. (2001). The postmodern turn in family therapy. *Christian Counseling Today, 1*(3).

Lyotard, Jean-Francois, (1982). *Postmodern Condition*, Geoff Bennington and Brian Massumi (trans.). Minneapolis: University of Minneapolis Press.

MacIntyre, A. (1984). *After virtue*, 2nd ed. Notre Dame: University of Notre Dame Press.

McLaren, B. (2004). *A generous orthodoxy*. Grand Rapids: Zondervan.

Middleton, J.R. & Walsh, B.J. (1995). *Truth is stranger than it used to be: Biblical faith in a postmodern age*. Downers Grove, IL: IVP.

Newbigin, L. (1989). *The gospel in a pluralist society*. Grand Rapids: Eerdmans.

Olthuis, James, H. (1990). A cold and comfortless hermeneutic or a warm and trembling hermeneutic: A conversation with John D. Caputo, *Christian Scholar's Review, 19*(4), 351.

Parker, I. (1992). *Discourse dynamics: Critical analysis for social and individual psychology*. London: Routledge.

Piehl, R. (2001). Narrative therapy and the Christian counselor: Necessary precautions. *Christian Counseling Today, 9*(3).

Sampson, E. E. (1993). Identity politics: Challenges to psychology's understanding. *American Psychologist, 48*(12), 1219-1220.

Shotter, J. (1993a). *Conversational realities*. London: Sage.

Shotter, J. (1993b). *Cultural politics of everyday life*. Buckingham: Open University Press.

Williams, R. (1992). 'Know thyself': What kind of an injunction? In M. McGee. (Ed.). Philosophy, religion and the spiritual life. *Royal Institute of Philosophy Supplement, 32*. Cambridge: Cambridge University Press.

Wolterstorff, N. (1983). *Until justice and peace embrace.* Grand Rapids, MI: Eerdmans.

Yoder, J. H. (1972). *The politics of Jesus.* Grand Rapids, MI: Eerdmans.

Chapter 3: Liberation from conforming social patterns: the possibilities of Narrative Therapy to aid the exploration of Christian spiritualities.

Richard Cook

About the author

While history was never of interest to me when I was at school, I have become fascinated with it as I have gathered some history of my own. I often share with students in our counsellor education programme, the insight that hit me during the BBC series, "Son of God". As the computer animation rebuilt the temple in Jerusalem, the presenter relayed that Jesus, from a humble town and background, would have come to the city and seen all the extravagance and performance of the Pharisees. The contrast, explained the presenter, would have been stark. My lifelong interest in the way ideas shape our lives coupled with this insight into the way Jesus' ideas were so radical in the milieu of his day, sparked the writing of this chapter. Its purpose is to show how Jesus liberated by offering an alternative story and that we too, in utilising Narrative processes, can be agents of liberation in our own day.

Conformed to the world

A cruel, murderous, persecutor of religious fanatics had an unsolicited spiritual encounter that changed his personal knowledge of spiritual life, and ultimately the name he was known by. Saul, later known as Paul wrote to the people of his home town urging them, "don't be conformed into the patterns of this world, but instead be transformed by the renewing of your mind so that you may find out what the good, acceptable and complete will of God is" (Romans 12:2). A more recent translation renders this saying as: "Don't become so well adjusted to your culture that you fit into it without even thinking. Instead, fix your attention on God. You'll be changed from the inside out" (Petersen, 2000).

This changed man had had firsthand experience of being conformed into the religious mould of the Jewish Pharisee sect to the extent that he was utterly convinced it was the only permissible version of spirituality and that "aberrant" versions needed to be eradicated. A strict code of behaviour and thought had been passed on to him in minute detail and he was intent on conforming those around him to the same code. Once he literally "saw the light", he could see how he had been squeezed and conformed to an oppressive set of knowledges. As a result of this insight he devoted his life as a Christ-follower to promoting resistance of that code of religious law, to the preservation and extension of people's personal liberation and to encouraging their spiritual connectedness with the founder of this resistance - the revolutionary Jesus of Nazareth.

Liberation

Liberation in Christian theology relates to three main aspects of life. The first is spiritual. Spiritual liberation is described as a kind of birth process out of the domination of self-centredness (sin), spiritual independence and malevolent spiritual forces. This birthing is into a new realm – the Kingdom (or leadership) of God where connection with the transcendent and eternal is discovered (John 3:1-8; Colossians 1:13; Romans 6-8). This leads to the second aspect, which is personal liberation – the gradual transformation of the disciple (learner) from the inside out. Here life-limiting patterns learned in social and familial contexts are gradually resisted and replaced by alternative ideas and practices (Matthew 23:26; Romans 12:2; 2nd Corinthians 3:16-18). Thirdly, liberation relates to engaging with injustice, inequality, oppression and cruelty in the social world. It is about struggling for social change and includes standing alongside those who resist these practices. It is about seeking to construct alternative communities and ways of being guided by ideas about justice, equality, kindness, respect and freedom that have circulated in Jewish and Christian communities (Deuteronomy 15:4; Proverbs 21:13; Isaiah, 58).

Liberation is also a theme in Narrative Therapy. Michel Foucault, whose writing was one of the inspirations for the development of Narrative ideas (White, 1991; Monk, Winslade, Crocket & Epston, 1997, p8), speaks of repression as the development of social rules (discourses) that proscribe what is acceptable in speech and action (Foucault, 1990). Among other things, he writes of how ideas about sexuality, for example, are negotiated in the social arena. He shows how these discourses have become defining of the experience and practices of sexuality in Western society over the last 200 years (Foucault, 1994). This has provided a process for analysing the way ideas actually construct practices and experience across all facets of personal and social life.

Foucault's process of analysis has inspired the Narrative idea of deconstructing the discourses related to whatever distress prompts a client to come to therapy. Deconstruction is the exploration of the ideas and rules embedded in social interactions that delimit acceptable thought, experience and behaviour in a particular context (White, 2002a; Freedman & Combs, 1996; Monk et al, 1997). The purpose of this teasing out of discourses is to help make visible the repression and oppression that is occurring since "dominant narratives tend to blind us to the possibility that other narratives might offer us" (Freedman & Combs, 1996, p39). Liberation in Narrative Therapy then, has to do with the gradual resistance of these prescriptive ideas (Stacey, 1997, 2001) and the gradual noticing of micro-moments of time where alternative ideas are inspiring preferred thoughts and actions.

As Freedman and Combs (1996) show, there are fields of experience that Foucault did not discuss in depth - and religion is one of them. Following Foucault, we can say that social ideas and prescriptions are constructing the experience and practices of religion and spirituality just as they construct the experience and practices of sexuality (Foucault, 1985) or illness (Foucault, 1975). Therefore, exploring oppressive expectations circulating in the language of Christian institutions including Christian families, the church and Christian literature, can lead to personal and social liberation. This is achieved by identifying alternative ideas and practices whose effects are life-enhancing.

Furthermore, this activity has a powerful precedent in the person of Jesus himself. The Christian scriptures record evidence of Jesus confronting and resisting the prevailing first century narrative of religion. That narrative held that God's acceptance was dependant on keeping up an outer appearance of goodness through a myriad of prescriptions for living. Such oppressive discourses were being circulated by the then ruling religious sect - the Pharisees. The radical Jesus protested and resisted these dominating strictures on the experience of spirituality. He articulated alternative ideas and practices of freedom, connectedness, equality, respect and genuineness. As such, he was mounting what Foucault called an "insurrection of subjugated knowledges" (Foucault, 1980, pp80-84) and proposing a "return of knowledge" – in Jesus' case, of a personal, liberating, compassionate, accepting and initiating God.

An example of this is found in the Christian scriptures in the account of Matthew, in chapter 23 and verses 4-12 of his writings:

> They tie up heavy loads and put them on people's shoulders, but they themselves are not willing to lift a finger to move them. Everything they do is done for men to see… they love the place of honour at banquets and the most important seats in the synagogues; they love to be greeted in the marketplaces and to have men call them 'Rabbi.' But you are not to be called 'Rabbi,' for you have only one Master and you are all brothers and sisters. And do not call anyone on earth 'father,' for you have one Father, and he is in heaven. Nor are you to be called 'teacher,' for you have one Teacher, the Christ. The greatest among you will be your servant. For whoever exalts himself will be humbled, and whoever humbles himself will be exalted. (Barker, 1978)

Here Jesus makes visible the power positioning (Monk et al, 1997) inherent in the dominant narrative: the religious "experts" held the power to place emotional and spiritual prescriptions on God's people. In order to be acceptable as "good Jews" they were forced to carry unjust and unrealistic requirements, without help from those whose role it was to serve them. Jesus protests the narrative of "the show", that is, being billed as "teacher" and taking the place of honour, believing it was fitting for their 'higher' position and knowledge. Jesus calls his followers to resist these ideas and the associated practices. He urged them to create an alternative community where equality, humility and service are the guiding ideas. In the alternative narrative it is not the power holders who are important; the esteemed are those who serve. This is an inverse power relationship.

As an associate of Jesus, Matthew records Jesus confronting the religious power-holders at another time, saying:

> Woe to you, teachers of the law and Pharisees, you
> hypocrites! You clean the outside of the cup and dish,
> but inside they are full of greed and self-indulgence.
> Blind Pharisee! First clean the inside of the cup and
> dish, and then the outside also will be clean (Barker,
> 1978: Matthew 23:25).

Here Jesus protests the dominant narrative that appearing to do the 'right' thing on the outside is the way to be confident of the grace of God. Like a postmodern, Narrative exploration, Jesus identifies the 'mechanism of influence' of this dominant narrative, the way this influence is wielded, namely coercing people to live prescribed lives but with their inner life untouched by a connection with the life of God. Jesus declares an alternative narrative: repentance (a change of knowing) happens when one's inner life becomes connected to God and this overflows in the fruit of a fully experienced and liberated life. As the ancient mystic Irenaeus later called it: the glory of God is a person fully alive! Similar to a Narrative process, Jesus advocates resistance to the dominant narrative. He calls for the adoption of an alternative narrative, one of genuineness and congruence, one that says, 'attend to the inner place first and then the outer life will follow naturally'.

In one further example we hear Jesus further deconstructing the narrative of obligation to external law-keeping:

> Woe to you, teachers of the law and Pharisees, you hypocrites! You give a tenth of your spices - mint, dill and cumin. But you have neglected the more important matters of the law—justice (fairness), mercy (compassion) and faithfulness (commitment). You should have practiced the latter, without neglecting the former. You blind guides! You strain out a gnat but swallow a camel (Barker, 1978: Matthew 23:23-24).

Here we see the law being imposed by the Pharisees on people's habits in the tiniest of things, their herb gardens. Jesus announces an alternative narrative: that being the people of Yahweh's story means much larger scale expressions of faith including being a people of justice, mercy and faithfulness. This was a story told about spirituality at earlier times in the Jewish history before the Pharisee branch of Judaism rose to their powerful domination of the faith.

At least two things can be said from reading these accounts. Firstly, Jesus has set a precedent for deconstructing life-limiting religious prescriptions. As a result, Christians can use Narrative explorations because their founder used a similar approach of deconstruction. Secondly, in the collaborative search for liberation, the obligation that Christian clients experience to be modern-day law-keepers of prescriptive religious narratives can legitimately be explored, just as narratives of gender, illness, family or relationship might be explored (Cook, 2000a).

At our time in history there is a great array of denominations and of Christian prescriptions for living. But there are also pockets of resistance of these prescriptions and a greater awareness of spirituality in broader terms. Recent New Zealand research such as Alan Webster's (2001) work shows the large number of people who have a meaningful belief in God (64%) but do not attend a Sunday institutional church. Alan Jamieson's work has shown the variety of spiritual journeys New Zealanders are on (2000). This seems to suggest that a number have abandoned the institutional organisation and are seeking spiritual insights and connections in a plethora of personal narratives.

So how might we be involved in this process of liberation as counsellors who are Christ-followers or as counsellors working with Christian clients? We can use a Narrative approach to deconstruct dominant Christian leadership discourse such as 'the Pastor knows' and, 'the Pastor is the pinnacle position'. The effects of this hierarchy of importance in the church can lead to people doubting their own knowing and lead them into a 'try-hard' approach in order to gain recognition for outer behaviour. These effects can be mapped out with clients during counselling. The prescriptions can be deconstructed. Micro-moments where clients have other knowledges of their acceptability by and their worth to God can be identified.

A restorying of Christian leadership as serving the needs of others as brothers and sisters on a journey (White, 2002b) opens the possibility of creating a community of respect, where the personal knowledges of each member and the mutuality of care is valued. Alternative versions of Christian spirituality have the potential to revolutionise the church: to flatten out the hierarchical structure, to esteem the giftedness of each other and to value the ways those gifts contribute to a community of reciprocal nurture. (This is discussed further in Chapter 13).

Narrative Therapy can also be used to deconstruct Christian discourses of obligation to do good works as 'good Christian performers'. This is a narrative that often produces effects like anxiety, trying hard and a sense of failure for Christ-followers. A new story can be pieced together drawing on times of connectedness to God. The restorying process can explore moments when a person sees what really matters to them and help them formulate their personal commitment to justice, compassion, equity and mercy. This process can facilitate genuineness and congruence between the inner and outer self.

The examples that follow illustrate some of the possibilities of this process with clients who identify themselves as Christians.

Some examples in practice

A woman in her mid-thirties had been experiencing recurring panic attacks along with a sense of failure and a dread of not measuring up. She described her extensive bookshelf of Christian self-help books and a general impression she held that she simply needed to try harder and be the person that her version of God expected her to be. She had heard the same message in some Christian circles and held onto a dominating story that an acceptable Christian has to be friendly, frequently winning others over to a Christian commitment and needing to change herself successfully to be the many things that 'an acceptable Christian woman' should be.

Counselling progressed over several months identifying the version of a Christian she was trying to live and the discourses inspiring that, such as, 'a good Christian should be friendly to all... should win many to a Christian commitment and should be able to beat anxiety or panic'. We mapped the effects of these discourses, the history over two generations and the position of 'the inadequate one' that the performance-training discourses (or messages) had placed her in. We saw, for example, how the discourse that 'a good Christian doesn't feel panic and should be able to beat anxiety' was itself stimulating anxiety about having anxiety. We listed out the many dictates of 'a good Christian woman' that she had internalised in her reading of self-help books and church interactions. We saw how these gave her a pervading sense of failure and falling-short. As Michael White describes, modern power has us keeping ourselves under constant surveillance and measuring ourselves against socially prescribed norms (2004). He shows how the distressing experience of failure signals an implicit longing for another way of being in the world – one free of the bullying of social dictates.

Gradually she identified glimpses of where alternative interpretations were inspiring a new story – that messages of Christian performance were stories of Western society and not of the founder of her faith. For example, she spoke of moments of feeling she was allowed to "sit in the sun with Jesus". These were moments where she caught glimpses of acceptability. A change of knowing dawned. In her words recently, "I got a new understanding of grace". These were initial steps in a gradual and ongoing journey that still needs many more conversations to thicken the plot line of the alternative story (White, 1995, 1997, 2000, 2007; Morgan, 2000).

The second example involves a middle-aged couple whose experience had included pastoring several churches and raising several children. A range of messages about performing as a Christian family had persuaded them that, "the children should all follow in the same path, be pure when they marry, stay married for life and come home for happy family occasions". When one of the children's marriages ended, these parents were distraught. Our conversation centred on their distress that the child did not fit what they saw was an ideal Christian family picture. That picture had developed in a church context where powerful messages positioned parents as successful if their children abstained from sex until their wedding day, were still together over time and seemed always to be happy. 'Failing' families then, were those where there was pregnancy before marriage, or separation or even the presence of conflict. As my own research suggested (Cook, 2000b), success and failure discourses can hold enormous power over family members and inspire anxiety rather than possibility dynamics.

This family said their journey involved smashing their 'ideal Christian family' picture in their minds. It was as if the picture frame lay cracked and broken and could never be mended back to an original design. Our work was to question the shame and failure messages that came from not looking like the ideal picture and to piece together an alternative version of a 'Christian family'. This meant talking through an alternative version of Christian spirituality and metaphorically leaving the pressure to 'fit the picture' with the broken picture frame on the floor. We wove together fragments of a grace-based theology with notions of the acceptance of God, of God working things out for good, of speaking personal truth and of weathering conflict and difference. They described a new picture emerging, one without poses. It was more of a 'candid shot': family members talking over coffee, others in a disagreement in the next room, kids telling parents about their frustrations with them and parents prepared to hear it. Interestingly, they did not want a constraining picture frame any longer. Their picture now did not have edges. It was inspired by a view of God as a parent, one longing for connection, but accepting the choices of His created children.

Conclusion

Jesus of Nazareth's only recorded attacks were on the power-holders of the day who had enslaved the Jewish faith to become the opposite of its design (Douglas, 1987, p779). They were purveyors of imperatives that enslaved people to external signs of goodness. Jesus deconstructed this 'discourse of externals'. He resisted and protested their power and made visible the positionings they imposed. He announced alternative narratives and offered alternative positionings that were revolutionary in the social world of his day.

Christ-followers today often come to counselling weighed down by expectations to be a certain way at home, at church, in society and within themselves. The messages that keep these clients ensnared are imbued with a supernatural authority because they seem so closely aligned to "God" – the supreme authority figure. Revelation of the socially constructed nature of these conforming messages can lead to a gradual liberation. This growing freedom offers an alternative view of Jesus and an alternative version of Christian spirituality – one of our connectedness to Love, a new knowing of fatherly acceptance and a collaboration with divine mercy.

Narrative Therapy is a way of exploring Christian spirituality because it can assist clients to identify social forces that are conforming them. It can aid the process of resisting these forces and coming to know personal and social liberation. That early follower Paul of Tarsus who had had genuine change of knowing, wrote another letter calling followers in the ancient region of Galatia to "stand firm and not submit again to a yoke of slavery". Followers of Christian spirituality often need to hear that today, and Narrative Therapy can assist.

References

Barker, K. (Ed.) (1978). *The new international version study Bible*. New Brunswick: International Bible Society/Zondervan.

Cook, R. (2000a). Christian narrative therapy. *The Christian Counsellor, 4: Jan-March 2000*, 30-34.

Cook, R. (2000b). *Discourses inspiring strengths in a selection of NZ families*. Unpublished Masters' thesis: University of Waikato.

Douglas, J. (Ed) (1987). *The new international dictionary of the Bible*. Hants: Marshall-Pickering.

Foucault, M. (1975). *The birth of a clinic: An archaeology of medical perception*. New York: Random House.

Foucault, M. (1980). *Power/knowledge: Selected interviews and other writings, 1972-1977*. New York: Pantheon Books.

Foucault, M. (1985). *The history of sexuality, Vol. 2: The use of pleasure*. New York: Pantheon Books.

Foucault, M. (1990). *The history of sexuality: An introduction*. London: Penguin.

Foucault, M. (1994). *The history of sexuality*. London: Peregrine Books.

Freedman, J. & Combs, G. (1996). *Narrative therapy: The construction of preferred realities*. New York: Norton.

Jamieson, A. (2000). *A churchless faith*. Wellington: Phillip Garside Pub.

Monk, G., Winslade, J., Crocket, K., & Epston, D. (1997). *Narrative therapy in practice: The archaeology of hope*. San Francisco: Jossey-Bass.

Morgan, A. (2000). *What is narrative therapy?* Adelaide: Dulwich.

Petersen, E. (2000). *The message*. Colorado Springs: Nav Press.

Stacey, K. (1997). Alternative metaphors for externalising conversations. *Gecko: A journal of deconstruction and narrative ideas 1*, 29-51.

Stacey, K. (2001). More than protest: further explorations of alternative metaphors in narrative therapy. *Australia and New Zealand Journal of Family Therapy 22*(3), 120-128.

Webster, A. (2001). *Spiral of Values: The flow from survival values to global consciousness in New Zealand*. Alpha Publications.

White, M. (1991). Deconstruction and therapy. *Dulwich Centre Newsletter 1991 No 3*, 21-40.

White, M. (1995). *Re-authoring lives: Interviews and essays*. Adelaide: Dulwich.

White, M. (1997). *Narratives of therapists lives*. Adelaide: Dulwich.

White, M. (2000). *Reflections on narrative practice*. Adelaide: Dulwich.

White, M. (2002a). Addressing personal failure. *The International Journal of Narrative Therapy and Community Work, 3*.

White, M. (2002b). Journey metaphors. *The International Journal of Narrative Therapy and Community Work, 4*.

White, M. (2004). *Narrative practice and exotic lives*. Adelaide: Dulwich.

This chapter was adapted from an article first published as:
Cook, R. (2003). Liberation from conforming social patterns. *Journal of Counselling, 24*(1), pp. 19-26.
Re-published with permission.

Chapter 4: Narrative and being free: a theological look at Narrative Therapy and implications for conceptualising human freedom.

Nicola Hoggard Creegan

About the author

I lecture in theology at the Bible College of New Zealand. I grew up in a scientific household and have long had a deep interest in a range of issues on the science/faith interface. My doctoral dissertation at Drew University in New Jersey was on the theology of human freedom and bondage, and I have since begun to look at these issues as they related to Narrative. I am also interested in spirituality and the theology of healing. I live in Titirangi with Charlie and two teenage sons. I have a BA (Hons) in mathematics and a PhD in theology.

Introduction

As a Christian theologian I have a long-standing interest in the theology of human freedom and healing, including ideas around our conditioning, motivation, enculturation, freedom of the will and responsibility. My encounter with Narrative Therapy came through the book, *Biting the Hand that Starves You* (Maisel, Epston and Borden, 2004) which discusses Narrative treatment for anorexia and bulimia (A/B). In this chapter I will discuss my growing conviction that Narrative Therapy is of enormous interest for spiritual and psychological well being.

In my doctoral dissertation, completed in the early nineties, I looked at the "grammar of freedom" using the work two contrasting historical figures, Jonathan Edwards and Friedrich Schleiermacher (Hoggard Creegan, 1992). Whereas these theologians represent opposite ends of the debate over liberal versus conservative theology, they both argue that there is no such thing as absolute free will; our actions are conditioned by our past motives, will and circumstances. Nevertheless both writers also argue that we are responsible. Jonathan Edwards is America's most influential theologian, a renaissance thinker, and preacher of the Great Awakening in the 18th century. Schleiermacher, known as the father of liberalism, is often associated with quite a different school of thought, that of liberal theology, and was the great modern theologian of the nineteenth century. As reformed theologians however, they agreed on the subject of freedom and bondage, that while there is no such thing as free will humans are nevertheless responsible for their actions.

I argued in my dissertation that although they have both presented this paradox of humans being conditioned and yet responsible, there is freedom in a more corporate sense, especially in the corporate nature of the church, which provides us with other ways of seeing, with hope, and with alternative narratives and metaphors by which we might understand ourselves; we come to transcend our brokenness and conditionedness or unfreedom by means of belonging to a corporate body. It is also interesting that with both Edwards and Schleiermacher the problem of freedom is approached in linguistic terms. The way we use the language of freedom and responsibility gives us a clue to who we are and to the kind of beings we are.

By the end of the dissertation, I realized that even I as the author was not quite convinced that humans could be considered responsible when I also knew they acted out of their enculturation and their conditioning. While I agreed with my conversation partners I realised nevertheless that the argument was largely not compelling to a more general audience. I was living in the United States at the time, and court case after court case brought home to me this conundrum of freedom and determinism--the whole riddle of responsibility in the legal sense continued to puzzle me. I often felt that the 'conditionedness' of the person entering into a criminal act was not taken into account. Harsh punishments were meted out as though each person reached a point of moral decision making completely freely and unimpaired. The long and turgid trial of Andrea Yates who drowned her children in a post-partum psychotic state is perhaps one of the keenest and most tragic examples.

The retributive nature of American penal systems resulted in huge injustices and inequalities, with many people suffering significant mental health problems in prisons. Young children were being incarcerated for life. These criminal cases raised questions which were pertinent to the "grammar of freedom" I had encountered. Andrea Yates would always *feel* responsible for drowning her children. The act itself resulted in a great tragedy and evil. Yet she herself was locked into a spiral of psychotic delusion in which all the significant people in her life let her down or made decisions which exacerbated the situation. She needed the help of others—as well as medication--to resist the voices which tempted her to destruction. She was anything but free in her delusions. The courts, however, treated her as a woman who had made a radically free decision, and tried her as such.[2] There was no compassion for her circumstances and no account taken of the culpability of all the persons in her immediate circle of friends and family.

In this situation even Edwards would surely have claimed that Andrea Yates was *unable* to do good and although she might feel responsible, she probably wasn't. However in less extreme cases both Edwards and Schleiermacher would argue that a person's conditionedness was compatible with some measure of responsibility. In this context my understanding of Narrative Therapy seemed to be consistent with this understanding of the "grammar of freedom" but also explained and filled out some of the puzzling gaps.

Narrative Therapy and freedom

Thus it was that I came to the reading of *Biting the Hand That Starves You: Inspiring Resistance to Anorexia/Bulimia* with enormous interest. One of the co-authors is David Epston, and his wife Anne is counsellor to a young relative of mine who has been in therapy for anorexia. I was surprised by the book, and the quite fresh approach

---

[2] After some years of incarceration Yates was acquitted on the grounds of insanity and is still incarcerated in a state institution.

to counselling it represented. I was surprised at the passion of the authors, and at the new insights it gave into human freedom and responsibility. I had heard of Narrative Therapy but didn't realize that externalization and 'co-research' were such significant factors in the approach.

Externalization was of interest because it is by this means that a person can resist the temptations of their circumstances, while not being defined within them, and not being totally at their mercy either.   Thus a person being tempted by anger or anorexia, or perfectionism or fear, can both admit that this is the condition in which they find themselves, but separate themselves from that condition by resistance and the recruitment of others into the struggle.

Externalization of oppressing voices interested me because it was in this way that the person achieves a measure of separation from the cultural conditionedness that produces problems. As Carl Hilker described it:

> Externalizing practices create a context in which problems are treated as separate from people. People are invited to discuss problems and constraints in a manner that separates them from these issues. This process is quite unique within a Western culture that values a scientific medical model that situates problems within individuals' biology and character (2007).

Madsen (1999) describes how Narrative Therapy portrays problems "as existing outside people as a linguistic device to reorganise our thinking in ways that counter shame and blame, minimize defensiveness, and promote client agency or the capacity to act on behalf of themselves in relation to problems." Externalization, then, effects a separation from cultural conditionedness, enabling a greater freedom to choose a course of action.

Another element that I was particularly interested in was "co-research." "Co-research" as a way of reframing the therapeutic process is a term used extensively by David Epston, and coined by him in 1989 (Maisel et al, 2004, p93). It refers to "the unmasking of A/B [which] takes place through an inquiry with the person struggling with it" (Maisel et al, 2004, p83). Epston's book and website are a resource for participative research into the tactics and arguments and seductions of the personified Anorexia/Bulimia (A/B). This has the therapist asking the client such things as: "what is Anorexia saying to you in this situation?" Co-research positions therapist and client as enquirers into how the cultural conditioning has been affected and how increasing moves towards freedom and agency have been achieved.

Narrative Therapy, then, identifies collaboratively the name of the culturally conditioned voice that is oppressing the person, and from that point it works at strategies for resisting this voice, for anticipating its revenge and for persevering in the long struggle for freedom from the voice. The client's natural supportive community or "life club" is seconded to help in this resistance.

I became convinced that this sort of therapy could be good for the whole person, and that perhaps it was the key that was missing in my previous explorations in freedom, and in my long puzzlement about the justice system. I was surprised in particular by:

a.   the remarkable passion of the therapists that went way beyond the in-hour time of consultation
b.   the very strong language associated with fighting A/B and recruiting the patient or client into the anti-A/B league.
c.   The theme of constant and unremitting deception by A/B being so pronounced
d.   The way in which externalization and co-research seemed to maintain the dignity and the freedom and responsibility of the person concerned.
e.   The connection between Narrative and social justice which is unusual given the private nature of the client/therapist relationship.

This left me with a number of questions/reflections. I was convinced that in this very powerful method Epston and White had "discovered" and had put into practice something analogous to the "grammar of freedom" I had uncovered in Schleiermacher and Edwards. The person is free and responsible, but in another way their freedom and power to act is conditioned. In spite of their situation, in order to be free and to be healed the person must "take" responsibility with the help of the "life club" to which they belong. This method resonates with and in another sense fills out the theology of conditioned freedom.

As I reflected on the Narrative method I realised that I had previously had half the story, and Narrative theory fills in some of the gaps. By externalizing the problem, the person is separated from their affliction. The essential human capacity, then, is not possessing a radical freedom, but the capacity to resist and then to build a different narrative. Only by taking control, speaking back, hating, and resisting the externalized hindrance does a measure of freedom and healing begin. This method takes seriously both the conditionedness of the person's situation, and the possibility of real responsibility for their own healing if others around them assist. Freedom becomes seen as a corporate possibility. This is reflected in the constant emphasis upon family support, upon the anti A/B league and on the support of one's "life club."

Further theological interpretations of Narrative

But Narrative also has puzzles. Who or what are the voices? Are they really just constructions of reality, or culturally conditioned responses? In my subsequent explorations I found a trinitarian interpretation of Narrative Therapy (Pembroke 2005). Pembroke, interacting with a number of others including Jacques (1991), argues that Narrative Therapy always involves "a tri-personal approach" (Pembroke 2005, p14) including the counsellor, the counselee and a "nurturing third" (Pembroke 2005, p16). The world is relational in trinitarian terms, and so it makes sense that community would be brought to bear on the problem of resisting evil. Together, moments of strength and resistance to the dominant, culturally determined narrative are highlighted and held strong. Only the community can lift these forgotten or passed over moments to a place of importance in the counsellee's life. The thinking of this paper was that we should not be surprised if freedom comes through community—that is the image of God in us.

Anther possibility is to see these voices as hypostases of the person, meaning those elements of the person that have a life of their own. In Christian theology we speak of the trinity as being one God and three hypostases. It is proper to talk of the life of the Son or the Father, yet they are one God.   The persons of the trinity are hypostases of God. There is some analogy with externalized voices. Fear, for example, is a good voice when there is danger. Perfectionism has its place in aiming for excellence. Given a life of their own, they become tyrannical and evil. This parallels the language of idolatry in the Scriptures. Idols are just parts of the creation that are good in themselves, but become works for evil when they are made ultimate instead of just having relative value. In this sense the voices are almost but not quite independent beings. Moreover, in the trinity there is a distinction yet not quite distinction of persons, a model also for the ambiguity we find in the externalized voice which depends for its existence on the person, but can be thrown out, away from that person.

Transversal dialogue

There are some resources in theology, then, that might shed light on freedom and being in bondage and externalized voices, but there are more critical conversations also happening in this area. Narrative Therapy is based, at least in theory, on a very constructionist, postmodern metaphysics. How does this relate to Christian faith?

Some help here might be gained by exploring method. In a recent book, *Alone in the World: Science and Theology on Human Uniqueness* - the 2004 Gifford Lectures - J. Wentzel Van Huyssteen (2006) develops a method of integration he calls transversal dialogue. This refers to the kind of discourse between disciplines that lays one against the other, but that does not attempt to reduce one side to the other, that quarries one language game for clues or resonance with the other. He uses this method to look at human origins in theology and in paleontology, anthropology and biology. The insights in one discipline resonate with and deepen an understanding in the other, but there is no false or premature conclusion—as there has been perhaps in the twentieth century in process theology which sees God as too close to the natural world, or in Deism in which God is remote from the world.   Transversal dialogue, however, does affirm an implicit belief that both are attempting to find the truth. Transversality seemed to explain what was going on for me as the insights from these two disciplines—theology of freedom and Narrative Therapy-- were placed alongside each other. The tension remaining in the ongoing dialogue of transversality can be the cause of more imaginative leaps and ongoing questions.

Externalized voices

A part of the tension for me in this transversal dialogue, was understanding the identity and nature of these externalized voices. Who or what were the voices of A/B? One writer in explaining this method to future therapists said:

> I have to give you a warning-- if externalization is approached purely as a technique, it will probably not produce profound effects. If you don't believe, to the bottom of your soul, that people are not their problems and that their difficulties are social and personal constructions, then you won't be seeing these transformations. When Epston or White are in action, you can tell they are absolutely convinced that people are not their problems. Their voices, their postures, their whole beings radiate possibility and hope (O'Hanlon, 1994, p28).

The language used in externalization is the strongest possible. At one stage David Epston, himself a Jew, draws a connection between the evil of the death camps and the voice of A/B (Maisel et al, 2004, p109). One has to outwit, hate, resist, and talk back to A/B. One can never be complacent. Even as the person returns to 'normal' the voice will come back in disguise. But if one really means it, doesn't there have to be something there? What imaginary externalized voice can be hated as much as death camp wardens? What constructed reality "talks back" and has such deception as this?

Yet this therapy emerges out of a post-structuralist, non-realist philosophy, based on people like Ricoeur and Derrida. Perhaps, then, Narrative therapists don't actually believe in the reality of these voices---seeing them rather as internalised values, concerns and obsessions of the larger society. In practice, however, these particular therapists really do believe in them and this is seen in how much they hate them and resist them passionately. Cameron Lee (2004) has published an article with just this critique, dismissing Narrative for these reasons, and claiming it is immoral because it is based on a postmodern philosophy, one that is suspicious of metanarratives, of truth and of reality. He suggests that poststructuralists seem to be playing games a great deal of the time. To me, though, this criticism of Narrative did not ring true. *Biting the Hand*, whatever its philosophical origins, bore the mark of moral intensity. These therapists were involved in a struggle between life and death, and they had no doubt at all which voice they should back.

Nevertheless at a deeper level I find myself also resisting the constructionist approach. We are, I think, too embodied, too much the result of a long evolutionary process to be living entirely in a world of our own imagining. Our circumstances and our cultural context and our significant family do deeply influence our sense of self and our story, but there is also significant biological and genetic input into who we are? Thus I am left with my puzzle about the nature of these voices. If the voices are not just constructs, what are they? Yes, the young woman might find herself in a society that values thinness, or in "problem-laden" stories, but her own biological and psychological makeup will contribute to the power these influences have over her.

The language of the demonic

I cannot help but notice that the grammar of this resistance mirrors closely the grammar of the old Christian vigilance about the Devil. On the other hand I would also resist an identification with the demonic, raising as it does an obsession with evil beings and with a whole historic mythology of the demonic which is probably unbiblical. It is interesting, though, that the fifth chapter of *Biting the Hand* is called "The Devil's Smile." The grammar of Narrative Therapy fits the language of temptation, used in even the contemporary church. This is biblical language. In biblical stories of healing Jesus drives out demons and calls upon the person themselves to resist their illness--to take up their bed and walk, to see again. Those healed must stop clinging to their ailment and take on healing and wholeness.

I wonder what resources there are in Christian theology for giving more life to these voices than mere constructions, however powerful constructions might be. I am thinking here of Walter Wink's insistence that we do live in a social/spiritual world dominated in some sense by powers and principalities. Wink would not wish to personify these as devils or angels but he does wish to give due biblical weight to the serious oppressive and deceptive force of these *powers* in our everyday life and in our institutions and social systems. Combining these ways of seeing gives new meaning to Joshua's call to "choose life." All life is choice. All human life is either resistance, choosing life, or acquiescence to these powers. Our capacity as humans to absorb the world in our minds, to transcend the world in our imaginations, to be malleable and to be adaptable also makes us vulnerable to deception and to temptation. Thus resistance is everything. But the temptations are a great deal more than the constructions of reality; in some sense the temptations have real spiritual power.

Jesus' temptation by the Devil is also of interest. Here the devil takes on the role of a friend, a wise counsellor, someone interested in Jesus' own welfare. This is the voice of the anorexia or perfectionism also, and carries with it the same implicit lie. In fact, lying and deception are taken for granted in Narrative Therapy. The person is not just led astray by a voice; it is a voice with an agenda, and coming under the guise of a friend. This is also a constant theme in Christian pastoral care. Deception always lingers around us in some manner, both personally and structurally. Deception is central theme in the Genesis story of our origins, and begins and ends the story of Jesus' adult ministry which begins with the temptation in the desert and ends with the Gethsemane agony of decision.

Thus Narrative Therapy has some intersections with spirituality, ones that resonate in the biblical and theological worlds. The language of conditioned freedom resonates with the real bondage Narrative Therapy assumes. Christian theology brings the language of the trinity's community of being as analogies to the communal nature of the resistance, and the powerful nurturing third party in any therapy. The language of hypostases within the trinity aids us in thinking of the quasi separation externalisation brings. But the intensity of the biblical engagement with temptation seems to do more than any other insight to locate the externalized voices as real; real in the sense of comprising a real part of the created/natural/cultural continuum, and real in the sense of being parts of this continuum that have the power to enslave; real in resonating so aptly with the life these temptations play within the biblical drama.

One cannot say they are imagined, or that they are distinct beings, or that they have come from somewhere else. But they are real and they are resistible as though they were alien. Narrative has stumbled on some deep truth of the human psyche, a truth which fits well with the biblical lifeworld. At some level these parallels work to flesh out the discourse between the disciplines of Narrative and theology. At another level the questions and differences remain and remain a part of a tension. The cross-disciplinary transversal tensions allow the introduction of Narrative Therapy into the realm of Christian discourse, thus giving it some orientation within that way of understanding the world.

For the Narrative practitioner I think this gives freedom in identifying and taking on these voices without having to imagine one is playing a game. The voices have power only because of the power of human language, but they are real nevertheless, even as the voices which tempted Jesus in the wilderness were real, and known as Satan. The ubiquity of such voices within the biblical drama should give us more confidence that this approach is justified. To the Christian practitioner, then, prayer can and should be added to the strategies for resistance and protection of the client.

Exocentricity

What is it though about the human person which gives us such expansive minds, minds that are able to construct and deconstruct narratives, minds that are vulnerable to deception and lies? Van Huyssteen believes that human brains are unique, but the uniqueness is in the opening up of the more sequestered intelligences which existed in the pre-human hominid brain. This opening up or fluidity of our brains gives us our special level of sentience, our self consciousness, our ability to use language to high levels of abstraction and opens us also to spiritual influence beyond the human realm. With brains like ours we can talk to God, and we can be deceived by other spiritual domains, and we can be used and enticed by the powers. Narrative Therapy at its best exploits this expansiveness of our minds while identifying and resisting the vulnerabilities which result from the same.

In theological language we can use the expressive term "exocentricity." This is a term used by Pannenberg to refer to that which is distinctive in the human being. Van Huyssteen explains:

> Pannenburg famously connects human nature and the imago Dei through the idea of 'exocentricity' a disposition that is intrinsic to the nature of human persons, and intrinsic precisely as a natural dynamic that points human beings toward a destiny that has not yet been reached. Exocentricty not only points to a human orientation to others and to the world, but in a much

more holistic sense reveals a disposition of human nature itself. Humans have this Weltoffenheit, or openness to the world, which by far transcends the openness of all animals to their environment. Exocentricity thus means that humans are always open beyond every experience and beyond any given situation, in fact beyond the world itself. We are even open beyond our own cultural constructions, as we transform nature into culture, and constantly replace earlier forms of culture with new ones, we are also open beyond culture to the future, and to our finding our ultimate destiny in the future. This restlessness of human nature forms an important root for all religious life (Van Huyssteen, 2006, p140).

This openness is a part of what presumably makes us human, and makes us vulnerable to oppressive cultural conditionedness. But when oppression has been resisted the openness frees us to be expansive, and able to go beyond even the finite and the "here and now"-- to be spiritual. The authors of *Biting the Hand* remark at the end of the book that it is those women who find a spiritual outlook who succeed best in persisting with their healing.

Spirituality

In summary, then, how does all of this relate to spirituality?

First, freedom. I have drawn associations between the corporate freedom I had postulated in a theological sense, and the resisting of oppressive voices that Narrative Therapy brings, together with an accompanying freedom in the new narratives and metaphors one can discover and create. Freedom in its widest possible sense of the word, is surely a mark of spirituality and mental health.

Second, healing. The role of being a counsellee has often been described as disheartening and disempowering. True, medicine might sometimes cure the body, but the cost in terms of dignity and disempowerment is often great. Narrative Therapy attempts to heal with dignity, freedom, empowerment and with social connection in mind.

Third, community. The theme of community arises often in contemporary discourse, perhaps because it is so elusive. Yet healing does not happen in Narrative Therapy without the healing corporate presence of others who will join in the verbal resistance of oppression, and will help in the uncovering of previous moments of strength and discernment. This is surely meaningful and a very connected expression of human community. Here I cannot help but think of the Australian poet and actor Alison Cassidy's poem, I heard first at a conference on mental health in Brisbane, "we were all closed in the same defeat" and, "judgment is simply trying to reject a part of what we are because of it" (McAuley, 2007). In Narrative Therapy there is a sense in which all those participating recognise the common clothing of defeat, and the common need to defeat the defeat.   Narrative Therapy through community works to bring judgment to those parts of us that hurt us.

Conclusion

In summary, I have brought Narrative Therapy and theological notions of corporate freedom and individual bondage into conversation. I have argued that Narrative Therapy, as exemplified in the book *Biting the Hand that Starves You*, has developed responses to the person "closed in defeat" which are biblical in the depth of their spirituality and resistance to evil, and also in the deliberate hopefulness involved in a shared resistance and shared rewriting the narrative of a person's life in more freeing ways. I have pondered the identity of the "voices" of oppression in Anorexia, for instance, and have noted the resonances with theological and biblical language of temptation and resistance. I concluded that these voices are real and evil, even if the philosophical basis of Narrative Therapy has been post-structuralist, not coming out of a biblical worldview at all. The spirituality of Narrative Therapy is life-giving, and an important contribution to being free in community. Churches would do well not only to adopt this as a method of counselling, but to adopt its insights and practices more generally in the life of the church and liturgy.

References

Hilker, C. F. III. (2007). *Making trouble for problems: Therapeutic assumptions and research behind the Narrative practice of externalizing conversations*, (Argosy University Ph.D thesis) Retrieved June 2, 2007 from http://www.narrativeapproaches.com/narrative%20papers%20folder/carl.htm,.

Hoggard Creegan, N. (1992). *The grammar of freedom: The bondage of the will in Jonathan Edwards and Friedrich Schleiermacher.* Drew University, Ph.D Thesis.

Jacques, F. (1999). *Difference and subjectivity.* (A. Rothwell, trans.). New Haven, CT: Yale University Press. (First published 1982)

Lee, C. (2004). Agency and purpose in narrative therapy: Questioning the postmodern rejection of metanarrative. *Journal of Psychology and Theology*, 32(3), 221-231.

McAuley, J. (2007). "Because" *Retrieved* August 21, 2007 from www.poemhunter.com

Madsen, W. (1999). *Collaborative therapy with multi-stressed families: From old problems to new futures.* New York: Guilford Press. (Quoted in Hilker)

Maisel, R., Epston, D. & Borden, A. (2004). *Biting the hand that starves you: Inspiring resistance to anorexia/bulimia.* New York: Norton.

O'Hanlon, B. (1994). "The third wave." *The Family Therapy Networker*, 19-29, 28 (quoted in Hilker).

Pembroke, N. (2005). A trinitarian perspective on the counseling alliance in narrative therapy. *Journal of Psychology and Christianity*, 24(1), 13-20.

Van Huyssteen, J. W. (2006) *Alone in the world?: Human uniqueness in science and theology.* Grand Rapids, MI: Eerdmans.

Wink, W. (1998). *When the powers fall: Reconciliation in the healing of nations.* Minneapolis: Fortress Press.

Wink, W (1999). *The powers that be: Theology for a new millennium.* New York: Doubleday.

Chapter 5: Power: A conversation between Narrative ideas and
Christian perspectives

Irene Alexander

About the author

My present work is to co-ordinate courses in counselling and social sciences at graduate and postgraduate level. I am the Dean of Social Sciences at Christian Heritage College where all our courses include Christian worldview ideas and a critique of secular theories as well as Christian perspectives. Both students and staff are constantly challenged to find truth not only through rational and evidence-based learning but also through relationship with God and personal self awareness and reflection of praxis. In learning Narrative Therapy we are seeking to follow Jesus who critiqued the dominant discourses of his day – especially the religious ones, and also to be true to the reality of what brings Life.

Introduction

One of the major points of conflict between Jesus and the religious leaders, was Jesus' challenge of power practices. He exposed the playacting of the Pharisees who did not practice what they taught, who accepted the places of honour, but whose hearts were far from God. He constantly tried to teach his disciples a different way of being by exposing their desire to take power, and by living consistently in servanthood. The tendency to power is ever subtle, and counsellors, pastors and teachers are not immune from using it although our relationships with power may be more complex. Postmodernism in general, and Narrative Therapy in particular, have explored power practices. This chapter continues the exploration with the intention of serving the counsellee more effectively.

Power and Narrative

Over the last few years I have become more aware of how my understandings of power profoundly influence how my relationships work and how my choices are made. While I would not have said that power was of particular interest to me in the first part of my life, I realise now that the way it affects relationships and decision-making is very influential. As a child I read the stories of Jesus and believed them, not appreciating until later how much of what was said alluded to practices of power. When Jesus said we are in the world but not of it I realised that meant I would not follow the ordinary path of career or money making. I thought I might be a missionary and live in Africa or India. I read stories of missionaries and was inspired by Jim Elliot who died trying to bring his God to the Auca Indians. As a result of this living outside the world systems I was not so pressured to conform to society's expectations to career and 'success' as many of my peers might have been. Of course there were other kinds of power that were invisible to me – that were only exposed later – I was deeply influenced by the power of expertise, believing at first, that teachers and lecturers know all. I also imbibed the power relations of gender and preferred a masculine way of knowing, believing it to be superior. My own preferences of relating however favoured co-operation and responsiveness rather than power-over. I was by no means comfortable with the labelling and incarceration of psychiatric patients and prisoners I experienced in my first employment in a psychiatric hospital.

It is not surprising then that I joined a missionary organisation which at that time eschewed hierarchy and encouraged young people to go anywhere and do anything with minimal training. Given my perspective as being different from the usual cultural perspective, it is not surprising that when I researched epistemology for my doctorate I became sensitive to different ways of knowing, gender differences and the privilege of expert power; or that I would be attracted to feminist writers who questioned practices of power and traditional male interpretation. It fits that I would be attracted to psychology, counselling and education relationships which emphasised each individual's unique world view, individual journey and personal understanding. Along with this, the Jesus I read of in the gospels was one who constantly challenged power, constantly questioned interpretations held sacred by those who held power, and consistently honoured the poor, the marginalised and the powerless, especially women.

Discovering Narrative Therapy I identified with the questioning of accepted social interpretations and ways of being, and with the inquiry into the power relationship of the therapist. I delighted in the deconstruction of society's or church's domination, devaluing of the marginalised, and hierarchical structures that favoured the rich and powerful. I favoured the critique of ideas that were accepted just because 'that was the way it was always done'. I saw Jesus, the disciples, Paul and the prophets as those who constantly chose to live another way.

Narrative Therapy and community work encourage the critique of power as an important part of the 'helping' process. Those who develop helping relationships have an implicit power relationship whether they are aware of it or not. Poststructural therapies seek to make more explicit the power practices of that relationship. Power practices refer to actions around power and the way the counselling and therapy relationship functions – who makes the decisions, whose expertise is used, who sets the way the relationship functions, the exchange of money and other 'rewards and affirmations' and so on.

> A Narrative approach pursues an 'analytics of power'.
> It seeks to uncover how, why, what and by whom knowledge and power are produced and negotiated in families, social groups, communities, institutions and society, either as mechanisms of social control or as mechanisms of social emancipation (Hancock, Epston and MacKenzie, 2006, p. 456).

As such a Narrative approach lends itself to unmasking power practices which may otherwise remain implicit and hidden.

Traditional power and the church's traditional power

Traditionally power has been understood to be more about possession of an entity, rather than about the quality of a relationship. Thus the person at the top of the hierarchy, or with the resources to reward or punish, 'possesses' power, and thus has power-over. Others lower down the hierarchy or without the resources do not possess power, or are 'powerless'. Implicit in this idea of power is that if one has 'more' power, someone else has 'less'. Thus if those 'with' power are to share it, they will end up with 'less'. This is the concept of unilateral power and "our sense of self-value is correlative to our place on the scale of inequality" (Loomer 1976, p. 14).

French and Raven (1960) outlined five kinds of power generally recognised in organisations and relationships – and which are recognisable in church history and structure. The first two kinds of power are similar, although they work in opposite ways. Coercive power is the ability to force someone to comply. Physical force may be used but other threats are also part of coercive power. Reward power relates to the person 'with power' having the resources to reward others - with payments, praise, or favours. The person with these resources can obviously withhold the reward. The basic currency is one of exchange – do what I want and I will give you what you want. Many in the Christian church have held a rather primitive view of God as a god of power – of reward and of punishment; coercing with the threat of hell or the ultimate incentive of heaven.

A third kind of power is legitimate power which relates to society's recognition of position - the power of government, the justice system, policeman, feudal lords. This is often a system of hierarchy - those further up the hierarchy have more power than those further down. Those immediately above us in the chain of command, or line management, are those we must obey. Those 'higher up' have the right to 'lord it over' those lower down. Many of our institutions – schools, armed forces, places of employment, prisons, and businesses

– are managed through a hierarchical structure. Through the ages the church has generally followed the practice of using hierarchy for control and organisation. Some denominations, for example the Quakers and the Brethren have been notable exceptions to this rule, believing that Jesus calls the church to a different practice of power.

Expert power is a different kind of power - that attributed to those with particular kinds of knowledge or expertise. Obviously education systems are rooted in this kind of understanding of power – as are many institutions in our society – medicine, psychotherapy, and consultancy. The church has privileged those with theological knowledge as having expert power; and health – including psychotherapy – has recognised those with training as experts who therefore can expect fees for services, and can be expected to advise and even direct.

The fifth kind of traditional power Frank and Raven (1960) identify is referent power, and, at least in the older definitions, also implied possession of power as of an object or commodity. It is the power one holds when others want to be in relationship, or favoured, or similar. Famous people, by definition, thus hold referent power. Charismatic people draw a following of those wanting to share the power exercised by their charm or influence. Referent power signifies being a reference point, and indicates perceived matching attitudes and values. Although relationship is implicit in referent power, there is still a sense of exchange of a commodity, rather than an understanding that power itself is relational.

The challenge from poststructural writers is not so much to deny these kinds of power, as to make power practices transparent. Thus Daphne Hewson (1999), a Narrative counsellor and supervisor, explains that an important part of the supervisory process is to make structural power transparent – for example, to recognise those who hold legitimate power, such as training groups and ethics committees, and outline their requirements for those she works with.

Traditionally the church has utilised all these kinds of power, and has assumed the right to that power. As a result power practices have not been made transparent. The linking of implicit power claims with spirituality has meant that many Christians have believed that pastors and other leaders speak with the 'voice of God'. Much spiritual abuse has resulted from these power practices, frequently with no such intention by those holding power. This is not meant to imply that these conceptualisations of power in themselves are faulty, but rather that assuming the right to power and not examining power practices leads to a culture of power-over which is not transparent, and which all too easily can become abusive. "When power is not permitted to be recognized or named, it cannot be negotiated or challenged" (Hewson 1999, p. 406).

Jesus' challenge of power

In contrast to much of church tradition through the centuries Jesus himself constantly challenged the religious hierarchy, leaders' assumption of power and his friends' understanding of personal power. Even his close disciples had difficulty grasping his perspective as it was so different from the prevailing mindset. It seems that the disciples very quickly understood and practised skills and processes most of us only glimpse fleetingly – healing, miracles, casting out demons. In contrast, they took years to comprehend Jesus' conceptualisation and practice of power. Right up to the last supper they were arguing about who was the greatest. Right up to that event, to the garden of Gethsemane, to the cross, Jesus was trying to demonstrate a different kind of power, a different kind of kingdom. In responding to their arguments about power positions Jesus said to the disciples, "The kings of the Gentiles lord it over them; and those who exercise authority over them call themselves Benefactors. But you are not to be like that" (Luke 22:25-26).

"You are not to be like that!" It is a different kind of power that Jesus is trying to teach the disciples. The kingdom is about serving, about empowering, about giving freedom. It is about influencing by example, about relating by invitation.

Jesus does not teach directly about power, so much as demonstrate the living of it in his relationships. He is consistently acknowledging power in others rather than accepting attribution of power ("Your faith has made you well") and he clearly shares power with the disciples early on in their relationship: "He appointed twelve - designating them apostles - that they might be with him and that he might send them out to preach and to have authority to drive out demons" (Mark 3: 14-15). In spite of their wanting to misuse power, for example wanting to call down fire from heaven (Luke 9:54), and their squabbling over rank and position (Luke 9:46, Mark 10:37 etc), Jesus deliberately gives them power and then debriefs them on their use of it (Mark 6: 30-31). He explains to them that the greatest should be as a servant – even as he is ("For even the Son of Man did not come to be served, but to serve" Mark 10:45). He clearly understood power to be something which increased rather than lessened, when it was shared. This is very different to an understanding of power as an object to wield, or a power that is unilateral. "When Jesus renounced the power of the world, it was [unilateral] power he forsook" (Nelson 1988, p. 101). Instead he demonstrated empowering.

Bennett Sims, of the Institute for Servant Leadership says, "The ability to empower is what makes great leadership a servanthood: it awakens the slumbering power in the souls of others" (1997, p. 33). Sims recognises that power shared actually increases its effect. He continues, "It is always the deep purpose of leadership to use power to call out the God-given power of others" (1997, p. 34).

This then becomes collaborative use of power rather than unilateral use, an empowering of others to make their own choices. The stark difference in these understandings came home to me in class one day when I was teaching about the different kinds of power and Jesus' conceptualisation of power and authority. A high-spirited young woman asked, "So how do I make people do what I want then?" I can imagine the disciples asking the same question, and Jesus answering them again – "It's not about making people do what you want; it is about serving them, empowering them, inviting them to make choices for the kingdom. You don't *make* them do anything. It's a different kind of kingdom."

The God who Jesus shows us is a God of invitation, of relationship, rather than a God of power over. A God who shares his power and calls out the power in us, rather than one who sets up structures with which to oppress those lower down the hierarchy. This Jesus who can stand before the Roman governor, the highest human authority in Jerusalem and refuse to answer him, until Pilate asks, "Don't you realize I have power either to free you or to crucify you?" And Jesus answers, "You would have no power over me if it were not given you from above" (John 18: 10-11). Jesus is recognising a different power system where it is not a question of power over which dominates or intervenes at whim, but rather the power that is within each of us. To me this answers the basic philosophical/ theological question, "How can God be all powerful and all loving? - the world proves he isn't." This question arises from a misconception of what God's power is like. It comes from an understanding of power that is power over – rather than invitational power, shared power, relational power. In his teaching and practice Jesus was thus opposing a power which did not line up with the power practices of the God he had come to reveal.

"How power is conceived of largely determines the options that are available to oppose its operations," says Michael White (2002, p. 37). Jesus had a clear understanding of the power systems that he was opposing. But like his disciples, many in the church have had conceptualisations other than what Jesus had and so have set up worldly patterns of power. Through history much of the church has taught a double message – that God gives us freedom, but that the church does not give the same freedom but uses power in a way that does not fit with the God who Jesus was incarnating. The church has tended to utilise traditional power which links with external rules around moral judgements.

An example of Jesus' questioning of traditional power can be seen in his response to the rules regarding the Sabbath. The more traditional centralised power system had rules regarding the Sabbath which he brought into question with his, "The Sabbath was made for people, not people for the Sabbath" (Mark 2:27, Today's NIV). Thus he questioned the central tenets of the religious system by opposing an external absolute law. The Pharisees had made rules about what specifically may and may not be done on the Sabbath. Jesus challenges these also with his question, "Doesn't each of you on the Sabbath untie his ox or donkey from the stall and lead it out to give it water? Then should not this woman (who was bent over with infirmity)... be set free on the Sabbath day from what bound her?" (Luke 13:15-16). He is introducing a whole new way of thinking about ethical judgements. The next section describes how a Narrative approach gives us a window into what this might be.

Modern power

The previous discussion has largely been around 'traditional power' as the church has utilised these kinds of power, and continues to do so. Traditional power establishes social control through centralised, institutionalised moral judgements which tend to be top-down, relating to particular groups, limiting and coercing, with very visible signs of power and mechanisms of surveillance, including exclusion. Michael White (2002) explores this conceptualisation of power, contrasting traditional power with 'modern power', drawing largely on the writings of Foucault. Much of society however has moved outside of the 'system' of centralised traditional power, and has become subject instead to 'modern power.'

Modern power, in contrast to traditional power, has become based in people's own thinking, using normalising judgments, exercised by people evaluating their own and each other's lives, according to continuums of normality/ abnormality and performance. The spotlight tends to be on individuals making them feel as though they are under public scrutiny by comparing them with norms and imperatives that shift depending on culture and context (White 2002). Michael White and David Epston (1990) explain that as a result people

> perpetually evaluate their own behaviour... we live in
> a society where evaluation and normalizing judgment
> has replaced the judiciary and torture as a primary

mechanism of social control: This is a society of the everpresent 'gaze' (p. 24).

The following contrast of these two kinds of power (summarised from White 2002), shows that traditional power is enforced from outside, whereas modern power depends more on individuals controlling themselves and their peers by constant normalising evaluation.

Traditional power	Modern power
Focuses on institutional morality	Focuses on norms and performance
Centralised	
Top-down	Pervasive, but subject to culture
Enforced from without	Monitored by the individual and enforced by the individual on the self and others
Highly visible	
Those who do not conform are punished or excluded	Implicit
	Everyone feels themselves to be under public scrutiny

In some ways Christians have resisted modern power which impels people to fit with society's norms, claiming that they are, for example, obeying 'Biblical absolutes'. What is often hidden for these individuals is that these 'absolutes' are also interpreted differently in various cultures and denominations. In fact their own culture and denomination is one of the 'shifting coalitions' Michael White describes as actually providing a 'norm' whereby their lives are measured. Indeed Christians are also subject to modern power in ways they have been less likely to understand because of their focus on a centralised power base – the church and the interpretation of the Bible. They have become, as Michael White suggests, the 'unwitting instruments' of this social control, "inside of the web of power relations of this system of modern power...that is particularly insidious and pervasive" (2002, p36), largely because they have not been aware of it.

Whereas traditional power acts through institutionalised moral judgement to prohibit, to limit, to restrict, modern power acts through normalising

judgement to constitute life – that is to form lives, to
fashion lives, to shape lives, or to manufacture lives
that reproduce the constructed norms of contemporary
culture (White 2002, p. 43).

The influence of modern power is thus much more subtle, being
implicit in television, film, magazines and the culture in which we
live and breathe. Working in a university setting with Christian
young people I have seen many examples of these students
'reproducing the constructed norms of contemporary culture,' for
example in their expectations of the female body image and of sexual
experience, their acceptance of consumerism, buying brand names
and so on. It is clear that Christians are subject to traditional power
utilised in many church settings, as well as to modern power,
implicit in the society which we inhabit. However from earliest times
Christian faith has explored a radical departure from subjection to all
these forms of power. The life Jesus lived particularly demonstrated
this.

Jesus' reinterpretation of many of the Old Testament rules could be
seen as a shift from traditional power to self-regulating modern
power. His questioning of the Sabbath rules could be interpreted as
an introduction to the modern power of a self-monitoring of
acceptable Sabbath norms. His references to Old Testament laws
with another interpretation could be perceived as a more stringent
set of norms by which to evaluate ourselves. For example "You have
heard that it was said, 'Do not commit adultery.' But I tell you that
anyone who looks at a woman lustfully has already committed
adultery with her in his heart" (Matthew 5:27-28). This is not the
centralised power and surveillance of traditional power, (apart
perhaps from the confessional) but gives the individual the choice to
self-evaluate. It has probably brought self-condemnation to millions
through the centuries, of those who interpret it as the self-judgement
of modern power. And here indeed is where the Christian religion
has become a vehicle for modern power, which, as Michael White
(1999) says, sets us up for personal failure. If the sayings of Jesus are
used for judgement of ourselves and others as a means of evaluation
and comparison, then indeed we are practising modern power just as
Foucault and Michael White describe. We have indeed become

subject to the policing and surveillance not only of behaviour, but also of our innermost thoughts, and we are constantly open to self-scrutiny. If Jesus were indeed passing down a religion of rules of moral judgement, as many church-goers have thought, then we are certainly enmeshed in a pervasive and insidious web. If we are caught in this way of being, this rendering of Christianity which assesses our morality by comparison and judgement, then we are living out the practice of modern power. As a result, counsellors and pastors would also be expected to be part of the enforcement of this evaluation and condemnation, reinforcing modern power practices.

This is not however how I have come to understand Jesus' motivation. John tells us that he came to bring us abundant life, and truth that sets us free (John 10:10, John 8:32), not, as many have thought, rules that constrict and repress and censure. So what then is Jesus calling us to? He says he has brought a new covenant, a new way of relating to God, a new way of right standing – of moral understanding. He is introducing a whole new understanding of power and of morality, of being 'made right' in God's eyes. He tells the story of the tax collector who goes home justified (made right, acceptable), because he knew his need of God. This was in contrast, in Peterson's (1998) version of Luke 18:9, "to some who were complacently pleased with themselves over their moral performance" – the Pharisees – who stood in the temple and said "I do this, I do that". Instead, Jesus said, it was "the taxman, not the other, who went home *made right* with God". It is the taxman, the failing one, the broken one, whose very weakness brings him into the presence of God. He was indeed 'poor in spirit', with a heart that longed for God, and who thus gained entry to the kingdom of heaven. The 'others' of us, the good ones, may wrestle back and forth with fulfilling the requirements. "You are the very ones who pass yourselves off as virtuous in people's sight, but God knows your hearts" (Luke 16:15, Peterson, 1988).

These sayings of Jesus bring us face to face with the conceptualisations of power and of morality, with questions of 'ethical work' and 'telos' which Foucault (1994b), and White (2002) explore. Foucault defines 'telos' in this way:

> Which is the kind of being to which we aspire when we
> behave in a moral way? For instance, shall we become
> pure, or immortal, or free or masters of ourselves, and
> so on? So, that's what I call telos (1994b, p. 265).

Ethical work is the attempts to transform ourselves into the telos – these aspirations. This is comparable to what Christians have traditionally called sanctification – becoming what we aspire to be, and the process whereby we seek to attain it. Too often this process has been much more like the Pharisees' moral performance than the taxman's falling into the hands of God.

Power and conceptualisation of morality

Michael White (2002) shows in his exploration of modern power that social control is practised through the individual policing of our own lives through comparison with continuums of normality/abnormality and formulae for ranking people in comparison with each other. Each of us has implicit expectations of ourselves and others informed by these social norms and formulae. This has become our moral code and our ethical work is the behavioural, intellectual and emotional work (Linnell 2004) we do to attain the telos, the endpoint. Michael White (2002), drawing on Foucault, points out that this does not necessarily imply conformity, but rather that individuals find their own way to respond to these norms. But as Cherubine (2005) points out this modern power "is often elusive, hidden, embedded into the familiar, taken-for-granted cultural practices of everyday life; hence it is difficult to unmask" (p. 135).

Christians as well as those of other faiths can be as unaware as those of no faith, of what these norms and formulae are. It is likely that we have absorbed familiar, cultural norms, as well as Christian religious norms which may or may not be related to the teaching and practice of Jesus. Indeed, over the last decade, I have been experiencing the unmasking of some of the 'modes of subjectification' Foucault (1994b) and Michael White (2002) write about – the ways in which I recognise myself as obliged to put into practice the implicit moral code I have adopted. As I have recognised that my attitudes and beliefs were all too similar to those of the Pharisees – that by fulfilling certain behaviours and moral practices I would make myself acceptable to God, that I would thus 'pass myself off as virtuous', that I could then be 'pleased with my moral performance' – my implicit telos was unmasked. In fact it was my failing to live up to these standards that was a key to their unmasking. As Michael White (2002) says, our conceptualisations of modern power lead us to personal failure, for example "failure to achieve desired ends in regard to personal development objectives; going off track in terms of one's goals for one's life.. unsatisfactory performances of one's assigned social role" (p. 45). It is the failure to achieve that can be the doorway to a freer life. He suggests that we need to abandon these goals, that in fact we may choose to resist the formulae for example by "a wilful abandonment of the pursuit of adequacy; an obstinate rejection of aspirations for the achievement of superior status" (p. 45). For me this sounds very similar to Jesus telling us that we are of another kingdom – and that we are in the world but not of it.

How then are we to conceptualise morality, ethics, and living a 'Christian' life? If we follow the route of traditional power we must submit ourselves to a central authority – the church, the Bible, the pastor – allowing these to have authority over us and to dictate to us our behaviour and beliefs. Many Christians would see this as no longer acceptable as a practice of their faith. In shifting away from these conceptualisations many have then adopted the more subtle modern power of comparison and self-surveillance, comparing themselves either with others from their church or denomination, or with interpretations of the Bible or religious codes of belief and action.

Foucault's exposure of modern power and modes of subjection can give us a window to see again what Jesus was trying to describe. Frequently Jesus used metaphors and parables as ways to break through the mindsets of his hearers: "The kingdom of heaven is like…" Many have understood this focus as being on life after death. Rather, I am convinced he was trying to give us a mode of being for the present life. The kingdom of heaven is like the prodigal father who came to intimate relationship with the son who failed badly; the kingdom of heaven is like the vineyard owner who paid the labourers far beyond what they expected; the kingdom of heaven is like the man who threw a feast for anybody who would attend. Our faith thus challenges us to examine what this means in our present lives, our everyday interactions with the people around us. How are we to live generously, extending grace as these parables demonstrate.

Foucault's (1994b) aim in unmasking modern power is that we may live "with as little domination as possible" (p. 298). Traditional Christian religion has often sought domination through external laws. We as Christians in a modern world have often lived as if our lives were meant to be under domination, a paradigm of evaluation, of self-policing, looking for any thought or action which does not measure up to a strict moral code. This is no longer how I see Jesus. I desire to take him at his word that we are to live freely, abundantly and in joyful relationship with God, ourselves and others. This is what I understand the kingdom of heaven to be. A mode of being where I live not under law, regulations, and moral impositions, but in an ongoing relationship with the creator God. A love-relationship in which I turn to the one who lives within me to bring freedom to myself and others – with indeed, 'as little domination as possible.' The final section of this chapter will explore this question further.

Narrative approaches, therapy and morality

In their commitment to as little domination as possible and to the analysis of power practices in therapy, Narrative approaches have particularly chosen a professional ethic of "collaborative inquiry and practice in which people are regarded as the authorities on their own experiences and realities" (Hancock et al, 2006, p. 456). It is recognised that therapists cannot be neutral in their work and that the therapist's position is a powerful one in relation to those seeking counselling. As well, that, "All therapy involves talking about problems that have been created and exist within relations of power and the politics of local culture. Therefore all counselling is 'political'" (Russell and Carey, 2003, p. 79). The Narrative approach then, chooses to be as transparent as possible about power, and is committed to a de-centred and influential approach (Morgan, 2002; White, 1997). De-centred because the person who comes to the therapist for consultation is recognised as the authority on their own lives and their knowledge and skills are put at the centre of the conversation. Influential because the therapist's expertise and therefore influence, is in contributing to the 'collaborative enquiry', in inter-viewing (Kvale, 1996) in such a way that the person's unacknowledged skills and knowledges are uncovered thus generating "fresh meanings, new knowledges and preferred realities" (Hancock et al, 2006, p. 456).

Narrative approaches thus choose to make power practices transparent in "the inherent power imbalance of therapeutic relationships" (Russell and Carey, 2003, p. 80). Thus "being transparent in our work about our values and beliefs is a further attempt to make it less likely that we will step into expert positions in relation to other people's lives (Russell and Carey, 2003, p. 79). In the past at least, Christians have been less aware of our tendency to impose our beliefs on others, and therefore we have been less transparent about our beliefs and values. Believing we are Right and guided by God, and that others need to accept our Truth, has made us less likely to examine power-over practices. Narrative and other post-structural understandings challenge Christians to become aware of our conceptualisations of power as well as our practices of power.

In his exploration of traditional and modern power, Michael White (2002) demonstrates that "modern power recruits people into the surveillance and policing of their own and others' lives" leading to the fashioning of our lives "according to the constructed norms of contemporary culture" (p. 44). This is our 'ethical work' and pursuit of transformation into the telos, the endpoint to which we aspire. Christians would call this sanctification and see part of our life work as becoming 'sanctified'. Narrative approaches can help us unmask our conceptualisation of the goal of sanctification, or telos, as well as our 'ethical work' - surely the same thing that Jesus was seeking to do in his teaching about the kingdom. Are we aiming to be like the Pharisees, complacent in our understanding of our own virtue, gained by living up to external rules? Or are we setting goals of righteousness surpassing those of the Pharisees as Jesus said to do? (Matthew 5:20). Many of us would hear this directive to mean higher moral standards, perfection of thought as well as action. If this is so then the telos of ethical work and personal surveillance will be something superhuman and unattainable. Certainly Jesus is talking about the heart, the inner life, rather than just behaviour. He makes it clear that he see actions and words as coming out of the heart. Have we heard this statement as the Pharisees would have – and try and make more rules? Or have we heard it with the ears of those in the grip of modern power and tried to self-evaluate to higher levels of performance? These possible responses need to be unpacked further since our understanding of what this means is the key to our conception of the telos of our faith.

The Pharisees took the commandments and reduced them to every single possible action. Keeping the Sabbath holy meant defining to the tiniest action what was work - which therefore could not be done on the Sabbath (can one light a candle? can one turn on a light switch?) Not committing adultery meant giving your wife a note of divorce before the sexual act with someone else. Tithing meant tearing the tenth of a mint leaf off before cooking with it. These were very careful explications of traditional power. Modern day Christians who have adopted a similar approach have become subject to modern power, which is demanding of perfection in thought word and deed; and condemning mistakes, failures and shortcomings as unacceptable. Jesus challenged both of these interpretations – not just because they were nit-picking, but because they missed the whole point of relationship with God. My own experience of failure has helped to unmask these systems of moral thought and has taught me that coming to God is not on the basis of evaluating whether I am good enough to come, whether I am virtuous in people's eyes – or God's – because of my moral performance. It is on the basis of God's love for me and my need - "Blessed are the poor in spirit [those who know their need] - for theirs is the kingdom of heaven" (Mathew 5:3). As Rilke puts it:

> But you rejoice in the faces of those who thirst.
> You delight in all who cling to you for life.

Learning to let go of performance and evaluation, to be poor in spirit, to grip God for survival, to fall into the arms of the Divine Mystery, bring a whole different conceptualisation of 'ethical work' – of God's expectations of my ways of being. It points instead to a way of being that is relational, accepting of weakness and failure, being vulnerable to others, and thus releasing them to be vulnerable, weak and 'in-process'.

How then does this understanding of ethics, of morality, of being acceptable to God on the basis of who God is, impact on conceptualisations of power? It relates to our understanding of how transformation takes place.

Transformational power and morality

Power-over is more about getting done what the one with power wants done. Social power that is based in position, coercion, reward and even expertise is more likely to be power-over and therefore is more about the person who supposedly holds the power, than the person who is the subject of it. If our goal is the transformation of people – whether through therapy, education or community work – we need to examine our beliefs about how power and influence bring about transformation. Power which requires certain behaviours in exchange for reward – whether that be approval, a qualification, wages, social inclusion – remains power over. Power which releases a person to their own choices with 'as little domination as possible' is influence, empowerment or power to. This is the power that transforms.

In his classic book *Leadership*, Burns (1978), compares transformational leadership and transactional leadership. Transactional leadership is based on a conceptualisation of power that involves exchange, the one with power gives reward, expertise, favour and social inclusion in exchange for the behaviour they require - similar to conceptualisations of traditional power explored above. Transformational leadership involves empowerment by the leader so that followers and employees develop and are transformed to be the most effective that they can be. This conceptualisation of leadership and therefore of organisational structure has influenced much innovation and empowerment in industry around the world.

Some writers suggest however that empowerment necessitates a hierarchical structure, for example Beckwith (1999) states, "the concept of empowerment would be meaningless unless there were hierarchical structures within which to empower" (p. 394), because the person with the hierarchical power can share that power only by virtue of being part of the structure. Kitzinger (1991) criticises this understanding of empowerment because it 'leaves the structural conditions unchanged'. Narrative approaches empower by making these structures transparent. I see Jesus as not only making these structures transparent, but stepping outside of them by not accepting their domination. Beckwith comes closer to this understanding when she suggests empowerment may be power-from-within.

A conceptualisation of power from within brings a whole new perspective to our understanding of power and influence. A mythical story which has been retold through the generations illustrates this well. A holy man is praying when a soldier bursts into his monastery. The holy man continues to pray, ignoring the intrusion. The soldier, weapon at the ready, gets impatient. "Don't you know I have the power to kill you!" he shouts. The holy man turns slowly and looks at him. "No," he says, "I have the power to let you kill me." This is power from within which chooses not to be dominated from power without.

When the people saw that Jesus "taught as one who had authority, and not as their teachers of the law" (Matthew 7:28-29) they recognised that he was demonstrating this kind of power from within, a power and authority that comes from an inner integrity rather than from position, resources or expertise. This is the power that influences by invitation, giving freedom. There is a moral imperative, a sense of recognition of embodied aspirations that inspires the onlooker in this kind of authority.

This is illustrated by the story Yancey (2001) tells of the partition of northern India into East and West Pakistan in 1947. "Mountbatten, a seasoned military commander, summed up his moral power with a simple strategic formula, at a time when civil war was breaking out across India" (p. 144). He had posted troops in the west, but Ghandi had strongly influenced people's choices to refrain from violence in the east. Lord Mountbatten is quoted as saying, "On my Western front I have 100,000 crack troops and unstoppable bloodshed. On my East I have one old man, and no bloodshed" (p. 145). This is certainly not power-over. And it is more than referent power which influences by people identifying with another. It is a deeper moral imperative - the influence of a man of authority who empowers others to act morally because of his choice to recognise a power from within as having priority over external power, even at great personal cost.

This is the authority that people recognised in Jesus. An authority that he showed in his response to Pilate. An authority that came, not from overturning the structures of the powerful people around them, but from not giving power to those structures, subject instead to a higher authority, another way of being, a different kingdom.

Sims (1997) points out that all power is an exchange of power. By this he is not referring to the exchange that happens when one person obeys another, and the one with power therefore gives reward. It is exchange in the sense that a powerful person does not have power unless the other somehow gives power, by agreeing to recognise that power. This may be obvious in the case of referent or expert power where we choose to accept the expertise or attractiveness of the other; or even in modern power - in the acceptance of the cultural norms by which individuals are evaluating themselves. But what the stories above show is that even coercive power, even the power of the gun, is not power unless the other person accepts it. The holy man chose not to attribute power to the soldier. Ghandi was appealing to a different way of being – he would choose death rather than violence. Jesus only recognised Pilate as having power because Pilate was given power by the Roman empire – and ultimately by God. Jesus lived according to his own choices whatever the Pharisees thought, and whatever the Roman governor chose to do. In so doing he called us to recognise a different kingdom, apart from the world's structures, a kingdom which is about choices and ethics and a heart towards other people rather than power-over.

The ethics of this kingdom are not about an imposed morality but are about freedom and choice and invitation. Marshall (2001) identifies Jesus' way of power and influence as power from within - as implicit authority. He uses the story in Luke 7:8 of the centurion who says to Jesus "I myself am a man under authority, with soldiers under me. I tell this one, 'Go,' and he goes; and that one, 'Come,' and he comes…" Marshall points out that the centurion does not focus on those under him to prove his power, but rather acknowledges that being under authority gives power. In the case of the centurion it was under the authority of Rome that gave power. But the centurion recognised Jesus' power as similar. Jesus' power came from being under the authority of God. What had he seen in Jesus' way of being that inspired his observations? He saw an authority that comes from living in integrity, being obedient to the kingdom in which one lives. By doing only what he 'sees the father doing' (John 5:19) Jesus enabled the power of God to flow through him. When he spoke the people intuitively recognised his authority – not like their teachers of the law. This is the authority that comes from a power from within, a relational power rooted in relationship with God.

Marshall (2001) explicates this dynamic further. He differentiates power practices that derive from different focal points of the person. Those who try to exercise power by their will tend to use dominating, power-over practices. Those who focus on the intellect use persuasion. Those who utilise emotion to influence tend towards manipulation. All of these can be experienced by the recipient as coercive rather than invitational, freedom-giving. Marshall terms these as 'soulish' rather than spiritual. He suggests that real authority is spiritual, and comes from the person being under the authority of God. The integrity of life is what creates the flow of authority which is what invites the other to respond - out of free choice rather than compulsion. It was this teaching that caused my student to ask, "But how can I make people do what I want?" She was recognising that authority from within actually invites the other – but never coerces them - in fact it lets go of 'making people do what I want'. This kind of power and authority from within only invites. Somehow it releases a moral imperative to be at work. So when Ghandi chose non-violence in the face of racism and religious bloodshed, his stance (backed by his own lifestyle and integrity) invited others to take a similar moral stance and live this out in their behaviour. In contrast to power-over, this kind of authority leaves the other to make a choice. It is a risky kind of power because it chooses never to force the other to respond. It demonstrates by example and then says either explicitly or implicitly, "Follow me." It is the kind of power that the God of the New Testament explicates. It is the kind of power that goes to death rather than dominates. It is a power which chooses seeming weakness rather than strength, domination and calling down legions of angels. Paul understood it when he said that God showed him that, "my power is made perfect in weakness" (2 Corinthians 12:9). I understand this to mean that God's kind of power is most effective, most complete, when I choose not to exercise power over, but choose instead a dependence on God which only invites the other to respond.

This being made perfect in weakness may sound very good in theory, but in practice what would it look like? I am finding that it means being willing to accept my own humanness, being honest about my flaws and failures. It is recognising that I do not live up to my own moral standards any more than other people do – but still seeking God's enabling to help me. As I am honest about these things, and allow others to see me as I am, I find that my weakness is what calls them to honesty and integrity. My acknowledgement of my own shadow allows others to acknowledge theirs. My willingness to be seen for who I am encourages others to see themselves more realistically, and each of us is thus enabled to freely respond to the God who calls us to freedom and abundant life. Admission of my weakness allows God's authority to flow, a power that gives choice to others so that we can learn to make moral choices which benefit others. It is a power that brings about transformation because it enables each individual to make the choices that come from their own 'power from within'.

This understanding of weakness and vulnerability fits with understandings of the use of self in therapy. Many therapists have noted the need for vulnerability and appropriate openness in the therapeutic relationship. Says Virginia Satir (2000), "Very little change goes on without the patient and therapist becoming vulnerable," (p. 23) and, "I have great respect for that deep level of communication where one really knows when and whom one can trust. I think it comes close to what Martin Buber called the "I-Thou" relationship" (p. 22).

Narrative approaches are very explicit about the political nature of the counselling relationship, and therefore about the choice of the counsellor to be in relationship which gives power to the other. Winslade, Crocket and Monk (1997) use the term co-authoring for this kind of relationship, "To us the term *co-authoring* describes a relational stance that we want to express in our actions and words..." (p. 54). They go on to relate co-authoring as directly recognising the *authority* of the other person:

> ...we prefer to speak of identity and personhood as emerging from conversations in social contexts, including the context of the counseling relationship. To be an author is to have authority to speak – especially to speak in one's own terms and on one's own behalf (p. 55).

Thus the sharing of power in co-authoring gives authority to the other, the person who is exploring and developing their own sense of themselves. This, I see, is how God co-authors with us.

The most challenging outcome of these understandings of power and authority is the challenge to our own transformation. It necessitates that I be willing to journey with another in such a way as to release the power within them. This is the outcome of my own choices to be in relationship with God, to allow God's responses to me and my need for change. It is my willingness to recognise my own weaknesses, my own poverty of spirit and to be committed to seeing the other as God sees them, accepting their faults as I trust God accepts mine. It is about choosing to have a heart that is towards them, for them, not standing in judgement of their failure to meet society's norms, or religious standards. Rather, trusting that their weakness and poverty of spirit will also bring them into the presence of the God whose power somehow flows from our willingness to be vulnerable and open.

References

Burns, J. M. (1978). *Leadership*. New York: Harper and Row.

Cherubine, M. (2005). Language, power and intentions: Some ideas for working with people whose lives are affected by substance abuse. *The International Journal of Narrative Therapy and Community Work, 3/4,* 131-139.

Foucault, M (1994a). On the genealogy of ethics. In P. Rabinow, (Ed). *Ethics: The essential works of Foucault 1.* London: Penguin.

Foucault, M (1994b). The ethics of a concern for self as a practice of freedom. In P. Rabinow, (Ed.). *Ethics: The essential works of Foucault 1.* London: Penguin.

French, J. P. R. Jr., & Raven, B. (1960). The bases of social power. In D. Cartwright & A. Zander (Eds.), *Group dynamics* (pp. 607-623). New York: Harper and Row.

Hancock, F., Epston, D. & MacKenzie, W. (2006). Forging treaty hope: The application and relevance of narrative ideas and practices in developing Treaty-based policy and practice. *Community Development Journal, 4,* 453-466.

Hewson, D. (1999). Empowerment in supervision. *Feminism and Psychology,* 9, 4, 406-409.

Kvale, S. (1996). *InterViews: An introduction to qualitative research interviewing.* Thousand Oaks, CA: Sage.

Linnell, S. (2004). Towards a 'poethics' of therapeutic practice. *The International Journal of Narrative Therapy and Community Work, 4,* 42-54.

Loomer, B. (1976). Two kinds of power. *Criterion,* 15(1).

Marshall, T. (2001). *Living in the freedom of the Spirit.* Tonbridge, Kent: Sovereign World.

Morgan, A. (2002). Beginning to use a narrative approach in therapy. *The International Journal of Narrative Therapy and Community Work, 1.*

Nelson, J. B. (1988). *The intimate connection: Male sexuality, masculine spirituality.* Philadelphia: Westminster Press.

Peterson E. (1993) *The message.* Colorado Springs, CO: Navpress

Rilke, R. (1899). *Du siehst, ich will viel.* Retrieved on 21 October, 2008 from http://rainer-maria-rilke.de/05a014ichwillviel.html [My translation]

Russell, S. & Carey, M. (2003). Feminism, therapy and narrative ideas: Exploring some not so commonly asked questions. *The International Journal of Narrative Therapy and Community Work, 2, 67-81.*

Satir, V. (2000). The therapist story. In M. Baldwin (Ed.). *The use of self in therapy.* (2nd ed.). New York: Haworth.

Sims, B. J. (1997). *Servanthood: Leadership for the third millennium.* Boston: Cowley.

White, M. (1997). *Narratives of therapists' lives.* Adelaide: Dulwich.

White, M. (2000). On ethics and spiritualities of the surface. In M. White, *Reflections on narrative practice.* Adelaide: Dulwich.

White, M. (2002). Modern power and the production of failure. *The International Journal of Narrative Therapy and Community Work, 3, 33-76.*

White, M. & Epston, D. (1990). *Narrative means to therapeutic ends.* Adelaide: Dulwich.

Winslade, J., Crocket, K. and Monk, G. (1997). The therapeutic relationship. In G. Monk, J. Winslade, K. Crocket, and D. Epston. *Narrative therapy in practice: The archaeology of hope.* San Francisco: Jossey-Bass.

Yancey, P. (2001). *Soul survivor: How thirteen unlikely mentors helped my faith survive the church.* New York: Doubleday.

Chapter 6: Narrative Therapy and Narrative Theology:
A Conversation

John Meteyard

About the author

I first trained as a molecular geneticist and worked researching childhood viral diseases before the call to work with people rather than test tubes proved too strong. In 1992 with my wife Janet, I accepted an invitation to be involved in church pastoral ministry in Brisbane, Australia. I quickly became aware of how under equipped I was to help people from the congregation with the wide variety of problem stories with which they struggled. As a result I commenced studying counselling with Christian Heritage College (CHC) in 1994. This was to be a life changing experience and twelve years (and a Masters degree in counselling and one in Christian studies later) I am still at CHC as a lecturer. This role allows me to indulge one of my areas of greatest interest: the conversation between counselling, theology and Christian spirituality. My interest in Narrative ideas began around six years ago when I began to seek other ways of working especially with the men I saw who battled against different types of sexual compulsions. In addition to integrating counselling and theology, I also love good food and the great game of rugby union. Janet and I have been married for 16 years and have two children: Lauren, 12 and Stuart, 10.

Introduction

The release of this book on Narrative Therapy from a Christian perspective is one indication of the growing significance of this approach to counselling. As Lee (2001) suggests Narrative Therapy has grown in influence over the last ten years to the point where it is now one of the most influential counselling approaches in use today. What some readers may not realise, however, is that the recent explosion of interest in Narrative Therapy within the field of counselling and people helping is part of a larger move towards an emphasis on narrative and story that is occurring in a wide variety of academic and professional areas. Herman, Jahn and Ryan (2005) refer to this evolving focus as the 'narrative turn' and note that the emphasis on narrative has spread far beyond its initial origins within the study of literature and now encompasses fields as diverse as sociolinguistics, communication studies, philosophy, sociology, media studies, and the study of organisations.

It is not surprising, therefore, that recent decades have also witnessed a growing emphasis on Narrative Theology amongst both theologians and biblical scholars. When considering this book it seemed logical, therefore, to include a chapter on this narrative turn within Christian thought and to ask the question of how might the growing emergence of a narrative discourse in theology assist Christians with an interest in counselling and the helping professions to also understand, appraise and engage with Narrative Therapy.

To this end, this chapter seeks to achieve two specific aims. First, it attempts to answer the apparently straight-forward question, "What is Narrative Theology?" Second, potentially more interesting question for Christians within people-helping profession, "How might Narrative Theology help us to fruitfully engage the practices and ideas of Narrative Therapy?" In this section I have suggested four major ways I believe Narrative Theology can be helpful for Christians interested in Narrative Therapy, while acknowledging that this is but the beginning of a conversation between these two aspects of narrative theory that has many other interesting and exciting possibilities that others, no doubt, will continue to explore.

Narrative Theology for Beginners

In the early 1960's the reform minded pope, John XXIII, convened the Second Vatican Council to discuss the spiritual renewal of the Catholic Church and the position of the Church in the modern world. John XXIII invited 60 delegates from outside of Catholicism to observe the proceedings of Vatican II. One of them was the 39 year old Lutheran professor of medieval church history, George Lindbeck.

From that time on Lindbeck devoted himself to the question of how best to approach ecumenism, and after twenty years published a book *The nature of doctrine: Religion and theology in a post-liberal age* (1984) in which he identified that the single greatest block to ecumenism could be summed up in one word - doctrine! He therefore attempted to develop a new approach to doing theology that he believed possessed the potential to bring Christians together rather than emphasising their differences. To this end Lindbeck advocated a 'cultural-linguistic' model in which the scriptural texts are understood as an interpretative framework within which communities of Christians can develop doctrines that then serve to guide and shape the discourses, attitudes and actions of those communities. Note then that in Lindbeck's approach doctrines are not 'first-order truth claims' as they are for many evangelicals, but rather communal 'rules for life' that arise from the encounter of different groups of believers with the stories of Scripture.

Narrative theologians including Hans Frei, George Stroup, and Stanley Hauweras have taken Lindbeck's emphasis on 'cultural-linguistics' one step further to explore how the biblical narratives themselves should be understood and how they might impact the lives of individual believers and their faith communities.

This statement begs the question, "What exactly is narrative?" As many writers have noted human beings have an almost universal tendency to tell stories about their lives and their worlds. As Miller and Grenz (1998, p. 206) explain there is something about being human that makes us want to believe that life is meaningful and not merely a chaotic and insignificant series of disparate events. Narrative or story-telling "fulfil(s) this need by linking the past and the future with the present, that is, by understanding the present in the light of the past and the future" (Miller and Grenz, 1998, p. 206). It follows, therefore, that the more success individuals or groups of people are in understanding the experiences of their lives in terms of coherent, overarching and meaningful stories the more integrated those lives will be (Novak, 1971).

What then is Narrative Theology? For a longer answer I would recommend Michael Goldberg's excellent *Theology and narrative: A critical introduction* (1982). My brief overview begins with one of the best known Narrative theologians of the past thirty years, Hans Frei and his seminal work, *The eclipse of biblical narrative* (1974).

Hans Frei was a long-term colleague of George Lindbeck whose growing emphasis on a 'cultural-linguistic' model for understanding doctrine was to have a significant impact on Frei's own theological interests and development. Building on Lindbeck's concerns that both conservative orthodox and experiential liberal theology possess inherent limitations, Frei went a step further, arguing that the approaches of both schools have actually resulted in the meaning of the biblical story becoming detached from its essential truth (Miller and Grenz, 1998). Frei believed that prior to the eighteenth century "Christians had thought of the grand sweep of the Christian narratives as defining the real world. The world is the place created by God, where... Christ came, the church was founded, and Christ will come again; and Christians made sense of their own lives by placing them within that story" (Placher, 1997, p. 345). However, Frei also believed that in the last two hundred years a "great reversal" has taken place and now theology tends to interpret the biblical story from the perspective of our world, time and understanding, rather than the other way around (Frei, 1974, p. 130).

Frei strongly proposes that believers take seriously the deeper purposes of the biblical story as it is written. He points out that, "There really is an analogy between the Bible and a novel writer who says something like this: I mean what I say whether or not anything took place. I mean what I say. It's as simple as that: the text means what it says" (Frei, 1987, p. 22). For Frei, when we move to either reduce the biblical story (and the stories within its story) to propositional statements of doctrine or historically provable facts (as conservatives are prone to) or begin to look for experiential and universal morals (as liberals often do), we cease to take the Scripture seriously as it was originally written. As Placher (1997) explains to do so is akin to reducing a classic novel by Dickens to a merely moral lesson about how not to treat the poor or to a history lesson concerning nineteenth century England during the industrial age. While aspects of both of these subjects may be present, to do so is to seriously limit what the story is really about and what it may truly say to us.

Similarly, Frei suggests that to be true to the Bible we must encounter it as a narrative in which the whole is greater than the sum of it parts. By taking seriously the unfolding plot and developing characters within the biblical story, we are able to gain insights and understandings about God, the human condition and the purpose of human existence that would otherwise be hidden from us (Miller and Grenz, 1998). For Frei, therefore, becoming engaged in debate about the Bible's historical accuracy or whether there is a 'right' way to interpret particular doctrinal issues is to risk missing the point. However, approaching the Bible as a coherent and uniform narrative allows the believer to make sense of his or her own life and experience within a context greater than one's self. As Frei himself explains:

> Though real in his own right, the atoning Redeemer is at the same time a figure or type of the Christian's journey; for this is the narrative framework, the meaningful pattern within which alone the occurrence of the cross finds its applicative sense. What is real, and what therefore the Christian really lives, is his own pilgrimage; and to its (the biblical story's) pattern he looks for the assurance that he is really living it (Frei, 1989, p. 64).

Frei also had a deep belief in and commitment to the relevance and importance of the Christian faith within the wider world. Placher goes so far as arguing that Frei's theology (and by association much of the Narrative Theology that has succeeded him) is primarily a 'theology of the Church'. In other words it, "first of all addresses the Christian community and invites that community to let the biblical narratives shape its vision of the world" (Placher, 1989, ¶32). In effect the Bible tells the story around which the Church gathers to understand itself and its place in the world.

Building on Hans Frei's influential theoretical and hermeneutical foundation for Narrative Theology, other Narrative theologians have taken up the task of applying this approach within specific contexts and to specific issues but they share one important feature in common. That is the deeply held belief that we remain truest to the original intent of the individual biblical stories and the Christian narrative as a whole, when we engage these stories holistically. In other words Narrative theologians advocate we engage the Christian scriptures as they are written for the purpose of personally and corporately being transformed by them.

Narrative Theology and Narrative Therapy

Although there are many different areas in which a conversation between Narrative Theology and Narrative Therapy could be of potential interest and value for Christian practitioners with an interest in Narrative ideas, I have decided to focus on four specific points of potential interaction that I believe have the potential to be the most helpful.

The centrality of story for understanding and working with people

The very first time I ever mentioned Narrative Therapy to a group of counselling students at the college at which I teach the response of one student was very telling. He said something to the effect, "Working with people's stories doesn't sound very deep". This comment illustrates a criticism of Narrative Therapy that I have heard several times since. From a theological perspective, can the use of stories in the process of encouraging personal growth and change be justified? It is at this point that I believe Narrative Theology makes one of its most important contributions to a Christian engagement with Narrative Therapy. Simply stated Narrative Theology's reclamation of the centrality of story to understanding God, human beings and the Bible provides by association a strong ontological basis for viewing Narrative Therapy as a valid and significant way of both understanding and working with people therapeutically.

At this point it may be helpful to introduce the work of pioneering theorists in narrative including Jerome Bruner and Steven Crites (1971). This group of authors argued that as human beings we organise and understand our experiences through the use of narratives. As Ruffing explains:

> (Human) consciousness, too, must be narrative in form, a result of our experience of ourselves in time. This temporality is experienced through the always inter-related model of past, present and future. Only the present actually exists, but it exists only in a correlative relationship to its past and future (1989, p. 68).

Many theologians with an interest in narrative suggest that people understand their lives through stories because the God in whose image we have been created is (amongst other things!) a 'storying God'. Stanley Hauerwas makes this point well when he says, "We are a 'storied people' because the God that sustains us is a 'storied God'" (Hauerwas, 1981, p. 91). Indeed, the coherency of the Christian scriptures largely lies in the fact that it tells the story of God's loving interaction with humanity from creation to consummation. In Bartholomew and Goheen's (2004) words, "God's story, the true story of the whole world" (p. 11). When considering all of the means in which God could have chosen to explain Himself and His purpose to us, it is important to realise that He primarily chose to do so through what Bartholomew and Goheen (2004) call the "unified, coherent narrative of God's ongoing work within his kingdom" (p. 11). It follows, therefore, that a theological approach that emphasises the role of narrative is, in no way, 'majoring on the minors'. It is in fact focusing on an extremely important facet of what it means to be human and on the way we are to understand God and our interaction with Him.

So, if we do recognise this strong ontological basis for the centrality and significance of narrative within human experience, what effect does this have on our understanding of Narrative Therapy as

Christian practitioners? Perhaps I would now say to my questioning student something like, "You're right that working with stories may not always seem to be that 'deep' or significant when first considered. However, that may have more to do with living in a church and wider culture that has, to a large degree, lost touch with how important stories actually are for us as people, than it does to the inherent significance of stories themselves. Indeed, the fact that God has chosen narrative as a major way of revealing Himself to us should say to us that when Narrative Therapy focuses on the individual, group and cultural stories which influence people's lives, they are in fact concentrating on something very deep and significant indeed!"

The importance of narrative in human identity

As any counsellor or person involved in the people helping professions will attest the issue of identity is amongst the most common causes that bring people through our doors to ask for our assistance. As Freedman and Combs (1996) explain, Narrative Therapy and the other constructivist approaches to working therapeutically with people have challenged some of the long-held ideas of the psychological world concerning human identity in recent years. Narrative Therapy has proposed that human identity is not an embedded, structural and immutable human quality. Instead, Narrative therapists argue that identity is better understood in terms of the stories we construct about ourselves in collaboration with those around us (Freedman & Combs, 1996).

While Hans Frei was instrumental in developing the hermeneutical and theoretical basis of Narrative Theology, those who have followed after him have tended to concentrate on applying Narrative Theology in specific areas of human experience. One example of such a theologian is George Stroup, a well-known professor of theology at Columbia Theological Seminary best known for his writing exploring the relationship between the Christian story and Christian identity.

Stroup believes that personal identity is largely autobiographical. In other words people develop a sense of 'who they are' as they interpret the events of their lives within the context of an "interpretative scheme" that may include such intangible elements as ideals, values, preferences and goals (Miller and Grenz, 1998, p. 207). For the Christian this interpretative framework is often provided by the Christian 'tradition' which has been told and told again over time by the faith community in which she or he lives. McClendon (1983) explains Stroup's theory regarding the development of a Christian "identity- narratives" as follows:

> These seem to be not so much actual stories, as the name might suggest, but self-understandings or self-interpretations that have some connection with memories from one's past...It is argued that Christian faith is created whenever one's "identity narrative" (that is, self-understanding) "collides" with the prototypical Christian narratives (p. 50).

These theologians are basing this claim (at least in part) on what they believe is the way God has revealed identity is to be constructed, whether this be His own identity or that of the Church.

As this suggests, Stroup holds that Christian identity has a strongly communal aspect. A Christian's self-understanding is shaped by his or her encounter with the Christian story, however, this story is best told within the context of a faith community that is held together by the narrative that they share and regularly tell to one another (Stroup, 1991). Thus when the church is faithful in narrating the biblical story the result is that people are able to helpfully construct and understand their individual identity narratives.

What then are the implications of such an understanding of Narrative Theology for a Christian engagement with Narrative Therapy? I believe that there at least three. First, Narrative Theology supports the role of narrative in the more specific construction of human identity. After all if the Narrative theologians are correct and narrative is God's preferred way of revealing His own identity to us then it follows that narrative can also play an important role in the formation of how people understand themselves at both the individual and communal level. Second, Narrative Theology's recognition of the importance of the community in helping construct identity is certainly consistent with the emphasis in Narrative Therapy in utilising co-authoring practices (e.g. re-membering, reflective teams, therapeutic letters and so on) to help 'thicken' the construction of our counsellee's preferred identities. Finally, Stroup's emphasis on the role that the biblical narrative, as told by one's faith community, may play in helping to construct Christian identity opens potentially powerful possibilities for practitioners working with Christian clients. Indeed a healthy and functioning Church community grounded in the stories of the good news about Jesus is capable of powerfully thickening the new and preferred identity narratives of individual members wishing to leave behind older and less satisfactory stories about themselves and their lives.

The importance of Narrative in human ethics

It should come as no surprise to Christians with an interest in Narrative Therapy that one of the most common criticisms levelled at this approach by Christians is that due its strongly constructivist foundation it may be used to support an almost 'anything goes' goes approach to personal morality. As Lee (2004) has noted this criticism is probably somewhat over-stated as Narrative Therapy does in fact take a strong ethical stance against the marginalisation of individuals and groups whose stories do not match the dominant meta-narratives of the cultures and societies in which they live. However, there remains a lingering concern amongst many Christians that from a Christian perspective not all marginalised discourses can automatically be considered ethically acceptable, nor all meta-narratives too quickly dismissed as being oppressive and worthy of resistance (e.g. Piehl, 1999).

A third area in which Narrative Theology may have a contribution to make to a Christian dialogue with Narrative Therapy is therefore in the area of human ethical choice. Significantly, it is in this precise field that a large proportion of the Narrative theological enterprise has been directed and without doubt the Narrative theologian who has made the largest contribution to a 'Narrative Theology of ethics' is Stanley Hauerwas.

Hauerwas, a colourful and outspoken individual, believes that the majority of Christian discussion and scholarship concerning ethics has made the fundamental mistake of ignoring the central significance of narrative for ethical reflection (Hauerwas and Burrell, 1989). In his significant book *The peaceable kingdom* published in 1983, Hauerwas develops a compelling argument that faithfulness to the Christian story leaves no choice but for the Christian community to participate fully in the public moral deliberations of its day. Indeed learning to be Jesus' disciples involves learning to "shape our lives on the basis of the Jesus story and embody the virtues proper to it" (Pinnock, 1990, p. 206).

For the Christian, character is also not supposed to develop in isolation. Like George Stroup, Hauerwas argues for the central importance of the Christian community in shaping the Christian life. For example, when discussing how believers develop character or an "ethic of virtue", Hauerwas suggests that the single most important task of the Church in the world is "nothing less than to be a community capable of hearing the story of God we find in scripture and living in a manner that is faithful to that story" (Hauweras, 1981, p. 3). Although it may be a slight over-simplification Hauerwas' approach suggests that when facing an ethical choice (for example how to respond to someone who is very different to us) it may be more useful to reflect on the story of the Good Samaritan than it is to cogitate on abstract ethical principles (Placher, 1997).

Ethical choices and dilemmas faced by our clients are common occurrences in the counselling room. At the moment, for example, several of my own clients are facing choices concerning whether they should remain in or leave their marriages, attempt to give up life-controlling habits, and challenge potentially controlling behaviour by the designated leaders of their congregation.

So how might Narrative Theology helpfully inform the practice of Narrative Therapy at this point? It may be much more helpful for me to ask my clients struggling with whether they can remain in a troubled marriage, to reflect on the question of 'which stories about Jesus speak to you right now?' rather than talk to them about the different theological abstractions concerning the ethics of divorce.

Second, Narrative Theology also suggests that the Christian community has an important role to play in forming a context in which we have, "our character formed appropriately to God's character" (Doak, 2004, p. 132). This occurs not when we 'hold each other accountable' to certain ethical standards and expectations, but rather when we faithfully recount to each other and live out the narratives that make the Christian faith distinct. Thus a much more helpful approach than asking a client 'what does your church believe and teach about this?' might be to ask 'who in your faith community has faced this type of choice and what might their story and experience say to you?'

Finally, Narrative Theology reminds us that unlike some more propositional approaches to Christian ethics there may be as many specific responses to specific ethical dilemmas as there are believers to make these responses. For Hauerwas (1983) this diversity of expression is something that should be embraced and celebrated by Christian communities because it allows us to continually expand our understanding of the many different ways that we may live while remaining true to our story as Christians.

Using the Biblical narratives in counselling

How counsellors may use the Bible when working with clients has been a hotly contested topic within Christian counselling for many years. Views on this issue have ranged from the explicit use of the Bible for the purpose of admonishing clients in the case of Jay Adam's nouthetic confrontation approach (Adams, 1970), to the more implicit construction and use of a 'biblical worldview' as a frame through which to evaluate which aspects of specific models may be integrated by the Christian practitioner (Crabb, 1977). Many Christian counsellors, especially those who do not work in specific pastoral or church contexts, may feel unsure of how to use the Bible within their practice, due to a desire to avoid what has often been seen as overly directive and manipulative approaches by some conservative 'counsellors' in the past.

Narrative Theology may offer another helpful contribution for Christians wishing to include a Narrative Therapy perspective within their practice. This relates to the valuing of the Scriptures by Narrative theologians, without necessarily imposing overly propositional and narrowly defined meanings to them.

Sauter (2000) recounts the famous story of theologian Adolf Schlatter in 1893 when asked by the Prussian prime minister whether he 'stood on Scripture?' Schlatter is reported to have replied, 'I stand under Scripture'. In other words Schlatter believed the best approach to the Bible was to "expose oneself to Scripture, to pay attention to what it has to communicate" (Sauter, 2000, p. 7). Sauter goes on to argue that this stance captures the essence of what Narrative Theology aims to do. The believer and faith community is encouraged to allow the biblical narratives to impact and transform them holistically. For example Ruffing (1989) explains how a spiritual director may help a directee by inviting him or her to 'stand under a story' from the Bible and allow it to speak to and shape their view and experience. The great advantage of such an approach is that it opens up a whole range of possible outcomes and interpretations to one engaging the story while still remaining true to the original life-transforming purpose of the biblical narrative. Doak (2004) explains that such an approach understands that the Bible "is not monolithic, but is rather a source of unity-in-diversity, admitting a variety of interpretations" (p. 128). Perhaps questions of this kind grounded in the Narrative Theology principle of 'sitting under the story' might include: 'As you consider this issue is there a biblical story that really seems relevant or significant to you?' and 'As you sit with this story, what is it that stands out or seems important for you right now?'

Narrative Theology and Truth

Perhaps the biggest area of controversy for many Christians (especially those with a conservative view of the Bible) within both Narrative Theology and Narrative Therapy relates to the issue of truth. The view of Piehl (1999) is a good example of this:

> The Narrative Therapy community's claims about the oppressive nature of metanarratives, from which their vanguard techniques issue, theoretically expel metanarratives from any positive role in therapeutic process. This condition creates problems for those therapists for whom a master narrative is authoritative - including Christian therapists (Piehl, 1999, p. 6).

This stance is not really very different to the criticism of Narrative Theology by some more conservative theologians who argue that it often lacks a firm commitment to the propositional and historical accuracy of Scripture (e.g. Henry, 1987). However most of the Narrative theologians I have read (including Frei and Hauerwas) were quite clear in upholding their belief in the historical truth of the central events of the Christian faith, namely the coming, death and resurrection of Christ on our behalf. However, there is certainly no doubt that most Narrative theologians also believe that the actual historical accuracy of Scripture is less important than whether a church considers and acts as though the biblical narratives are actually true and authoritative.

As Hartt (1989) has indicated the key question for Narrative Theology, therefore, is not is this or that biblical story true (i.e. historically accurate), rather, the question is does it possess *verisimilitude* (i.e. 'likeness to truth'). The view of Karl Barth, one of the best-known theologians of the twentieth century, is a good example of this approach. Barth regarded the story of Jesus as a divinely authorised narrative in which the truth concerning human history has been made evident. For Barth what was of most importance for us is the fact that we can trust the biblical story to tell us rightly about God and about ourselves (Jenson, 1997).

For Narrative theologians then not all stories or narratives are of equal weight. Most do believe there is a fundamental difference between ordinary stories that entertain or instruct us in everyday matters and the biblical narratives that are divinely instituted for a specific purpose. To quote Bartholomew and Goheen (2004):

> There are a great variety of stories. Some merely entertain us; others teach us what is right and good or warn us of danger and evil. But there are also stories that are basic or foundational: they provide us with an understanding of our whole world and of our place within it (p. 18).

This is of course the area in which Narrative Theology differs most significantly from Narrative Therapy. As Parry and Doan (1994) explains one of the core assumptions of Narrative Therapy (and other constructivist approaches) is that all narratives or stories should be considered to be of equal validity. This is obviously quite different to Narrative Theology that privileges some stories (including and often exclusively the Christian story) over other stories. Many Narrative therapists would presumably have difficulty with such an approach due to the oft stated belief that when some stories are privileged over others, the stories of those who don't fit within the dominant narrative tend to be marginalised and minimised. Indeed, even a brief consideration of the history of Christianity tragically reveals that the Christian story has been used on many occasions to support a wide range of oppressive practices including racism, anti-Semitism, sexism, slavery and imperialism (e.g. Placher, 1997). It is important, therefore, that if we are to agree with Narrative theologians about the place of biblical narrative as a sacred story that is not inherently oppressive, but can serve to helpfully inform and guide all of life, that we take time to understand the heart of the story as God has given it to us.

How then do Narrative theologians see this story? William Placher summarises Frei's understanding of the Christian story as follows:

> The world is a place created by God, where the Lord rescued Israel from Egypt, Christ came, the church was founded, and Christ will come again; and Christians make sense of their own lives by placing them within that story (Placher, 1997, p. 345).

We then live out this story through our faithful commitments to one another and to non-violent social action in the world. For Hauerwas, trusting that God is ultimately in charge means that we do not have to defend ourselves from the challenge others pose to our stories nor do we need to violently foist our stories onto them (Doak, 2004).

In summary then it can be said that Narrative theologians are not primarily interested in whether the Bible contains propositional or historical 'truth' (although many would agree that it does). Rather they believe that the Bible contains divinely authorised narratives which are truthful representations of how we can understand God, ourselves and how we are to live as Christians. Indeed the individual biblical narratives can be understood to collectively form a single overarching story possessing at least one (but possibly a number) of consistent and distinctive themes. How then might such a view contribute to our discussion on the use of Narrative Therapy by Christian practitioners?

Personally I believe that such an approach may go a long way to providing a solution to the oft repeated concern from Christians concerning the potential for 'moral relativism' within Narrative Therapy. If we agree with the position of most Narrative theologians that the Christian story represents a divinely authorised narrative then it also follows that not only is this Story (properly understood and applied) not inherently oppressive but it also has the potential to be profoundly liberating (e.g. Lee, 2004). Such an understanding corresponds closely to that of Middleton and Walsh (1995) who argue that the Christian master story is like a *pharmakon* (i.e. a drug that can act as a medication or a poison), in that it harbours the potential for both oppression and justice, violence and healing. Middleton and Walsh also argue, however, that the very nature of the Christian story (especially key elements including the suffering, oppression and ultimate liberation of God's people) actually, "incline the Christian story toward delegitimating and subverting violent, totalitizing uses of the story by those who claim to live out of it" (p. 87). If this really is the case it follows that the biblical narratives have the potential to assist clients who possess a Christian faith in both the deconstruction of existing problem saturated narratives and the reconstruction of new, preferred and life-affirming personal stories.

Conclusion

In conclusion it is my argument that Narrative Theology has the potential to helpfully inform Christians with an interest in incorporating Narrative Therapy within their practice. Specifically, incorporating the Narrative Theology view of the biblical narratives as divinely privileged stories through which we can understand and live our lives may address the concerns some Christians have about the potential 'moral relativism' of Narrative Therapy while still remaining true to its basic principles.

It seems to me that such an approach may go some way to simultaneously balancing three important concerns within Christian counselling. First, it may allow the biblical narratives to provide an important and privileged place within therapy should the client so desire. Second, it could potentially do so in a way that respects the inherently narrative nature of much of Scripture and of the Christian story as a whole without reducing it to propositions or doctrinal absolutes. Finally, it could allow those with whom we work to engage the biblical narratives in a way that opens up a wide variety of possibilities concerning how they might actually interpret their own lives and experiences within the broader vision of these stories while still remaining true to the Jesus' story as a whole.

As an illustration of this possibility I would like to conclude by briefly sharing a recent chapter in my own unfolding story as a follower of Christ. Around five years ago I entered a particularly difficult and challenging time. My wife of twelve years had recently come to a place where, to be true to her own faith journey, she felt she needed to lay aside the Christian faith she had followed since childhood and give herself space to ask questions and consider other possibilities.

After an initial period of blissful denial I found myself catapulted into a place of uncertainty and questioning myself. Suddenly that which had seemed so certain – marriage, family, church, faith and doctrine – had become unpredictable and insecure. The surety and steadiness of my wife's Christian commitment had long provided me with reassurance and confidence in my own faith and this was now gone.

I remember that one of the most difficult aspects of this time was my own sense of guilt that I, a 'mature' Christian of more than twenty years, could be experiencing such 'doubts'. Surely I, of all people, was supposed to know what the truth was and what I should and should not believe. Old church tapes about what would happen to 'back-sliders' played relentlessly in mind.

Fortunately I was a member of a Christian community that allowed me to be present to my doubts and uncertainty without judgement or pressure to find easy answers. One day I was having a Narrative conversation with one member of this community in the presence of a reflective team. This companion asked me what image best described what I as experiencing. I found that answer presented itself readily. I was a small boat in a storm, tossed relentlessly by the waves, unable to find peace or a way forward. The experience was so real that when I closed my eyes I felt my body sway unstoppably from side to side and nausea grip my stomach. He then simply asked me which story of Jesus resonated with me most at this point in my journey. Again the answer came readily: the disciples on the Sea of Galilee when a violent storm struck without warning. Suddenly I was Peter or John or Thomas as they feared for their lives on a voyage that had unexpectedly become dangerous and unpredictable.

My friend's third question was, "As you look around you what captures your attention?" This time the answer took longer to present itself. I looked at the sky and saw nothing but storm clouds; the sea presented only towering waves and spray; and there was no comfort in the disciple's terror and helplessness. Finally my gaze fell upon the figure in the back of the boat. There lay the Lord sleeping calmly in the midst of my storm. All at once I was overcome by a profound sense of peace. I heard myself say out loud, "He's so not worried!" In that moment my perspective changed forever. I saw that my guilt and anxiety was due to having been recruited by the narratives of my Christian community that preached certitude and a doubtless faith. Jesus however was different. He was comfortable in the middle of my storm of doubt and fear. Indeed he was right there with me in the boat.

I cannot really express the peace this realisation brought me. Suddenly I knew that this storm was not something to fight or run from. It was an adventure that needed to be faced and lived as millions of other seekers had done down the centuries. Minutes before I had thought that being a disciple of Christ meant forcing my questions down, now I knew it meant living them courageously with his help.

Five years later I have largely emerged from my storm although now the sea I sail on is far less calm, sure and predictable than it once was. I find I have fewer sure answers than I once did; however, this is more than balanced by a deeper love and trust in the Lord who is prepared to journey with me in my frailty and 'unknowing'. In the words of Narrative Theology I have discovered that the Christian story is far broader and encompassing than I had ever realised and is more than able to hold the developing thread of my own story within its spacious and trustworthy stream.

References

Adams, J. (1970). *Competent to counsel: An introduction to nouthetic counseling.* Grand Rapids, MI: Zondervan.

Bartholomew, C. G. and Goheen, M. W. (2004). *The drama of scripture: Finding our place in the biblical story.* Grand Rapids, MI: Baker.

Crabb, L. (1977). *Effective biblical counselling.* Grand Rapids, MI: Zondervan.

Crites, S. (1971). The narrative quality of experience. *The Journal of the American Academy of Religion, 39,* 291- 311.

Doak, M. (2004). *Reclaiming narrative for public theology.* New York: State University of New York.

Freedman, J. and Combs, G. (1996). *Narrative therapy: The social construction of preferred realities.* New York: W.W.Norton.

Frei, H. W. (1974). *The eclipse of biblical narrative: A study in eighteenth and nineteenth century hermeneutics.* New York: Yale University Press.

Frei, H. (1987). Response to "Narrative Theology: An evangelical appraisal". *Trinity Journal, 8,* 21- 24.

Frei, H. (1989). Apologetics, criticism, and the loss of narrative interpretation. In S. Hauerwas and L.G. Jones eds., *Why narrative? Readings in Narrative Theology* (pp. 45-64). Grand Rapids, MI: Eerdmans.

Goldberg, M. (1982). *Narrative and theology: A critical introduction.* Nashville, TN: Abingdon.

Hartt, J. (1989). Theological investments in story: Some comments on recent developments and some proposals. . In S. Hauerwas and L.G. Jones eds., *Why narrative? Readings in Narrative Theology* (pp. 279-292). Grand Rapids, MI: Eerdmans.

Hauerwas, S. (1981). *The community of character.* Notre Dame, IN: University of Notre Dame Press.

Hauerwas, S. (1983). *The peaceable kingdom.* Notre Dame, IN: University of Notre Dame Press.

Hauerwas, S. and Burrell, D. (1989). From system to story: An alternative pattern for rationality in ethics. . In S. Hauerwas and L.G. Jones eds., *Why narrative? Readings in Narrative Theology* (pp. 158-190). Grand Rapids, MI: Eerdmans.

Henry, C. (1987). Narrative theology: An evangelical appraisal. *Trinity Journal, 8,* 4-20.

Herman, D., Jahn, M. and Ryan, M. L. (Eds.) (2005). Narrative turn. In *The Routledge Encyclopaedia of Narrative Theory.* London: Routledge.

Jenson, R. W. (1997). Karl Barth. In D. F. Ford (Ed.)., *The modern theologians: An introduction to Christian theology in the twentieth century* (pp. 21-36). Boston, MA: Blackwell.

Lee, C. (2004). Agency and purpose in Narrative Therapy: Questioning the postmodern rejection of metanarrative. *Journal of Psychology and Theology, 32* (3), 221-231.

Lindbeck, G. (1984). *The nature of doctrine: Religion and theology in a postliberal age.* Philadelphia: Westminster.

McClendon, J. W. (1983). More on narrative. *Theology Today, 40* (1), 49-53.

Middleton, J. R. & Walsh, B. J. (1995). *Truth is stranger than it used to be: Biblical faith in a postmodern age.* Downers Grove, IL: IVP.

Miller, L. and Grenz, S. J. (1998). *Fortress introduction to contemporary theologies.* Minneapolis, MN: Fortress.

Novak, M. (1971). *Ascent of the mountain, flight of the dove.* San Francisco: Harper and Row.

Parry, A. & Doan, R. E. (1994). *Story re-visions: Narrative therapy in the postmodern world.* New York: Guilford.

Piehl, R. (1999). *From Narrative Therapy to Narrative Theology.* Unpublished doctoral dissertation, Fuller University.

Pinnock, C. H. (1990). *Tracking the maze: Finding our way through modern theology from an evangelical perspective.* San Francisco: Harper and Row.

Placher, W. C. (1989). *Hans Frei and the meaning of biblical narrative.* Retrieved 12 December, 2005, from http://www.religion-online.org/showarticle.asp?title=15.

Placher, W. C. (1997). Postliberal theology. In D. F. Ford ed., *The modern theologians: An introduction to Christian theology in the twentieth century* (pp. 343-356). Boston, MA: Blackwell. .

Ruffing, J. (1989). *Uncovering stories of faith: Spiritual direction and narrative.* New York: Paulist.

Sauter, G. (2000). 'Scriptural faithfulness' is not a 'scriptural principle'. In G. Sauter and J. Barton eds., *Revelation and story: Narrative theology and the centrality of story* (pp. 7-28). Sydney: Ashgate.

Stroup, G. W. (1991). Theology of narrative or Narrative Theology?: A response to *Why Narrative? Theology Today*, 47 (4), 424- 432.

Wright, N. T. (1992). *The New Testament and the people of God.* London: SPCK.

Chapter 7: Narrative, Suffering and the Alternate Story

Irene Alexander

About the author

Having worked as a psychologist and educator for three decades now I have been constantly challenged with the question of what enables people to grow and change. My work has been mostly but not wholly in a Christian context, which allows me to explore the integration of spirituality and psychological change. I have recognised in Narrative Therapy a number of principles which I believe fit with Christian understandings and which nurture the positive growth. I have become particularly interested in how a person's experience of suffering can help the transformative process, and how we understand that in psychological and spiritual perspectives.

Introduction

As a counselling educator and as a Christian I am frequently challenged with psychological ideas and counselling practices and how they match with the teaching of Jesus and is ways of bringing healing to people's lives. I have noticed in my own life how my experience of pain is frequently a catalyst to bring about change and growth, I have pondered on the reality of suffering and its redemptive value – not that suffering in itself brings redemption but that it is frequently the site of transformation when it is brought into the presence of the God who knows suffering. I have also tried to explain to students why I see Narrative Therapy as not another cognitive therapy but a holistic process which focuses on emotion as the point of identifying values and even spirituality. This chapter explores the Narrative process of unearthing the alternate story as a very Biblical transformation process.

The Alternate Story

One of the important contributions of Narrative Therapy to counselling and psychotherapy is the very positive emphasis on the alternate story (White, 1995). Since Freud's focus on psychopathology, defence mechanisms and neuroses, counselling has had a strong theme, if not central focal point, of uncovering negative causal factors, labelling pathological behaviour and identifying destructive processes. While hearing and acknowledging the problem story, a Narrative therapist is always on the lookout for the alternate story, the often unnoticed story of the counsellee's survival, strength and practices which have enabled them to fight back and even overcome.

The process of uncovering the alternate story is one of carefully sifting the past for practices and events that showed the counsellee's patterns of coping, rejecting domination, refusing oppression, beginning anew (White, 1995; Morgan, 2000). As the alternate story is uncovered the patterns are noticed and developed into a landscape of identity – an alternate identity that crystallises the reality of the person's ability to survive and flourish. This uncovering the alternate story is likened to an archaeological dig by Monk, Winslade and Epston (1996) – the careful, often painstaking process of brushing away the dust and rubble that cover the real artefacts beneath. In fact they subtitle their book on Narrative Therapy *An Archaeology of Hope*, drawing attention to the fact that in uncovering the past patterns, a person is grounded in hopeful possibilities for the future.

One of the most powerful experiences in recognising this process was hearing Michael White (2003) recount a therapy session. He recounted listening to the story of a woman trapped in a relationship where chronic domestic violence was present, and to which she continually, despairingly returned. He listened to this awful story of the present relationship, as well as the past - an alcoholic and abusive father, other violent relationships – unmitigating negativity – waiting for the inkling of an alternate story. The story went on and on with flat emotion and no sign of hope, and then there was the tiniest hint of emotion in the recounting of witnessing a road accident where a child was hurt. For most of us, this event, and the woman's reaction of shame and not being able to respond, would have been further evidence of her problems and helplessness. But no, this was the turning point in her story, the indication of a deeper story. How did Michael White keep searching, listening for this glimmer of hope? For me it indicated the very hope-filled, faith-filled process of Narrative Therapy. "Here is a man of faith!" was my response. I am not referring to faith as in believing certain doctrines or dogmas. Rather, faith in the human story, faith in the alternate story, faith that hope would somehow be uncovered.

The problem story was a recounting that over and over bad things happen, you can't do anything about it, and you can't be blamed for that. The alternate story began with this tiny indicator of shame at not being able to act when a child was hurt. Michael explored the reaction of shame, what was the shame about? She said she believed you should be able to protect or at least respond when a child is hurt. When had she believed that before, or been able to act on it? No memories of that. Would somebody else in her life know that she thought that way? No. What about when she was a child with her alcoholic father, would any of her siblings know she thought that? And then the memories began. As a girl she had been the one to hide her siblings from her drunken father. When she heard him coming she would hurry them away from the house to a hiding place. She would keep them there, having an intuitive sense of when it might be safe to return. What other stories were there of this kind of action? And so the alternate story was built – a little girl who so cared for her brothers and sisters that she would hide them from her drunkard father. A little girl, a young woman, a mother who wanted to protect children. The alternate story thus uncovered, became a story of hope that action *could* be taken to defend against violence – and the woman was at last able to recognise in herself one who could take action, and so was able to leave the violent situation.

Listening for the alternate story is a process of hope, a response of faith that – in my terms – there is a God who is present in the darkest of times, who can, with the choices of the person concerned, turn suffering into gold. Men and women of faith have long known that walking with the Divine Other is not simply reframing a difficult situation. Faith actively changes the difficulties, the storms, the fire, into possibilities of forging courage, strength and alternate pathways.

The Bible is made up of stories of men and women who are weak, oppressed, overlooked, threatened, imprisoned, enslaved – who become princes, wise ones, leaders: Moses, a failure shepherding sheep in the desert, who became the liberator of a nation; Saul, small in his own eyes but in God's a potential king; Esther the daughter of an oppressed people who became the Queen of a heathen nation; Joseph, slave and prisoner who became prime minister; Daniel and his young friends, exile servants who became advisors to Nebuchadnezzah king of Babylon; Mary a village girl who became the mother of the Christ, Saul a murderous Pharisee who became a self-giving evangelist. All of these became influential men and women not through power but through turning the story around, using the suffering to develop trust in a God who is present.

Indeed the Greatest Story is an alternate story. The story of a child born in a stable in an oppressed nation, his parents fleeing into exile to save his life. Growing up under tyranny, accused of insanity by his brothers, threatened by the religious authorities, misunderstood by his closest friends, betrayed, tortured, killed. And somehow God uses this story to demonstrate his coming to us, his solidarity with us, his extravagant and reckless love. Core to the Christian faith is the theme of life-death-life. Our God is a God who knows sorrow, grief, betrayal and death, and yet has turned these into a story of love, grace, joy and life. He is the God of the Alternate Story.

Suffering as an indication of values

So how does this process play out in practice? How does the alternate story fit with the practice of counselling in a Christian context? First and most importantly I believe it affects the stance of the counsellor. If we are men and women of faith we hold a faith-filled position that the fingerprints of God will be present in this person's story. Not that we will necessarily refer to God in the process. Indeed sometimes Christians are too quick to attribute to God what should rightly be attributed to the person themselves. We can too quickly disempower people, weaken their God-given freedom and agency by crediting God with their choices and consequences. Rather it is a stance of faith that looks for the positive. Again we can learn from Narrative Therapy here, in acknowledging that it is important to listen to the problem story first.

Often Christians are too quick to look for the positive, too ready to gloss over the pain of a person in need. This can be the result of a desire to prove that God is a good God, or it can be an outcome of their own fear of facing the reality that Christians are not immune to the suffering of the world – that indeed bad things happen to good people. The Alternate Story is not afraid to hear the problem story – for embedded in that story will be the seeds of hope. The Christian Narrative therapist hears the pain and negatives, holding to the hope that God is present and can transform – but searching with the person in their own story for their own experience of that. Men and women of faith should be the most able to take the time necessary to hear the pain of the other, knowing that nothing is ever beyond hope, no person beyond redemption. And being able to sift with patience through the destruction to find the tiniest indication of another story, a possibility of gold.

The earlier story gives an example of the process of this. The counsellor listens to the story of pain. But listens with faith, looks with the eyes of hope for indications of something different. Frequently a negative emotion is the indicator. A person's pain or anger often points to a value that has been violated. In the story above, the woman's shame was the first glimpse of her strong valuing of protection of children. If we will patiently explore the negative feeling we often can discover the value to which it is linked.

A woman whose story I witnessed was sharing the pain and shame of her marriage breakup. She said it was like riding a wild horse – all she could do was hold on, not knowing where she would end up. My colleague asked her if she had other stories of riding wild horses. She recounted several incidents from childhood through to the present of standing up for what she believed in, even though it cost her in various ways to do so. As they explored the stories together, she realised that her wild horse ride was the result of holding to two very strong values – which had become mutually exclusive. One value was for a lifelong marriage. The other value was for life-giving relationships, and a refusal to live long-term in a relationship of criticism and destructiveness. After years of choosing the first value at whatever cost she had opted for the latter. The wild horse ride was the result of her own and others' reactions to making that choice - when it meant letting go a value that she, and they, held as almost absolute. As the outsider witness identified the woman's courageous choices, and as together they identified the value she was standing for, she was able to see the theme of the alternate story – choosing life, choosing to stand up for a core value at whatever cost. Her ongoing pain at the ending of her marriage pointed to the strength of her values, and so to the alternate story of integrity rather than betrayal.

This story illustrates the alternate story process. In the midst of the story of pain and shame the woman shared a vivid picture – clinging on to a runaway wild horse. What is the value expressed in this image? The patient exploring of examples clarified the theme. Here is a woman who holds on to what she believes in even though it is like a wild horse ride. Even though she is in a minority. Even though it costs her career and status. This is a woman of integrity not duplicity.

The counsellor is not making value judgements. The counsellor is lending her expertise and patience to notice the glimmers of difference, to notice and explore the places of powerful emotion and what they are linked to - and so to uncover what the landscape of identity looks like.

Another example may serve to illustrate – again where a more explicit 'Christian' value has cut across another deep value. A middle-aged woman had agreed to have her elderly father come and share her family's home. But to her embarrassment and shame she found herself hardly able to speak when her father joined them for a meal. She found herself constantly resenting his intrusion. As the story of Speechlessness was explored, several stories unfolded. One was that as an adolescent the woman had chosen to go against her father's wishes in a very small matter. The values of honesty and respect seemed to be in question. But the young woman, usually honest and respectful, had refused the father's demand even though she could not explain why. Shamed by him, she still refused. When I asked her what her refusal might have been about, she was able to identify her attempt at independence, her small stand to be her own person. She then recalled several other examples where she had stood up to her father, even though he shamed her, and even though she could not explain her stand to him. She could identify in these examples why she had stood against him – it concerned protection of her family and protection of her own conviction of what God was asking of her. As the stories wove into a narrative, the landscape of identity showed a woman who was strong in her own independent convictions, but who had learned early that she was to honour her parents – and for her that had seemed to mean she was unable to speak out her disagreement. She recognised that her speechlessness had to do with the patterns of her life. But, more powerfully, she could see that she had chosen to stand against a domineering parent even though she believed she was required to 'honour' him by not disagreeing. Speechlessness was the result. When I last spoke to her, her voice was returning.

This conversation demonstrates how exploring the stories of pain and shame can reveal the person's unrecognised but precious values. It also shows how easily, explicit, so-called 'Christian' values such as honouring parents, can obscure and even obstruct other values that are equally important to the person, and which can in fact, be shown to be equally 'Christian' but are maybe more subtle – choosing life-giving relationships, choosing an individual identity. Narrative processes can help Christians to step outside the box of legalistic demands to which we can too easily give lip service. The process of externalising and seeking the alternate story frequently brings a whole new perspective.

Jesus was the master of the alternate perspective. In story after story he turns the tables on his accusers – and his friends. God's interest is in your heart motive rather than who you give taxes to; the Sabbath is made to serve humans not vice versa; you need to work out your own reactions to spiritual authority before you expect me to tell you of mine; we are going to Jerusalem towards the threat, not away from it; I will take on the role of a servant even though I could take that of Master; leave her alone – she can pour out a year's wages of perfume if she so chooses, to name but a few. The One who almost always questioned the status quo, especially the use of power, has a two thousand year old family who constantly insist on doing things the Right Way, on creating hierarchical structures and hiding the mistreatment of the oppressed. Christian counsellors have all too often thought that their role was to reinforce what the church hierarchy demanded, have used the Bible to demand certain explicit behaviours, have stuck to the traditional interpretations. Narrative processes help us to question the usual way of seeing things, help us to go towards the pain and shame to find the heart-felt convictions of those who come to us for understanding.

In his essay on the "Absent but implicit" Michael White (2000) gives examples of using a person's stated hurts to find the implicit positive beliefs and practices. In one story he explores the counsellee's idea that 'life just isn't fair' to find the counsellee's implicit value which gave acknowledgement to childhood maturity and learnings. Another of White's stories tells of exploring a man's childhood experiences of rejection and discovering his true motive of care as a father. A third story of a young woman's self-abuse turns to her deep sensitivity around injustice towards herself and others. These stories illustrate the discovery of alternate stories by searching for implicit values and earlier experiences of those values. Again the illustrations highlight ways to step outside the box of usual interpretations, and negative explanations. It is in going towards the pain with a sense of hope of an alternate story that the story is indeed found.

Freedom from the normalising gaze – and condemnation

Another gospel story illustrates most clearly the way Jesus first deconstructed societal perceptions as an important part of the process of healing. A woman is brought, a law is quoted, "Teacher, this woman has been caught in the act of adultery. Now in the Law Moses commanded us to stone such women. So what do you say?" (John 8: 4-5). Jesus, in an intentionally de-centred way, deconstructs the destructive power of the Law. While all the others stand around him he upsets the stances of power by bending down and writing in the sand. He slows the process, he changes its direction, and he refuses to be caught by an oppressive mindset. The listeners don't understand, they press him. He articulates a whole new way of seeing. "If this interpretation of the law – that all must be perfect – works for you, then you can use it to condemn." As he again bends and upsets the balance of power, they withdraw. The dominant, oppressive mindset is exposed and thus loses its authority. "Does no-one condemn you?" "No-one Lord." Here is the essence of the gospel – the new covenant – a whole new perception of God, "Neither do I condemn you." God, after all, is not a Law-Giver who demands perfection. His focus is always the individual not the system. So the woman, caught by a system which is now exposed, is released into a whole new way of seeing herself and her life. "Go and sin no more". So often this last phrase has been used to re-instate the destructive system just exposed. As if Jesus is saying, "You got away with it this time, don't take the risk of getting caught again," rather than, a much more Narrative way of seeing, along with Hebrews 8:10-13, "The old covenant is now obsolete, your heart is freed to a whole new way of being." The Narrative process deconstructs the oppressive mindsets, exposes the old legalisms, sets free to follow the intentions of the heart and the practices that bring freedom and life.

This story can also serve to explore the process of the normalising gaze. In exploring Foucault, White (2002) demonstrates that our current moral system has less to do with black and white systems of right and wrong, and more to do with a comparison with cultural 'norms'. I believe modern Christianity is influenced by both, a conviction amongst many evangelical Christians that the Bible gives a black and white unchangeable set of right and wrong behaviours and a more subtle imbibing of the modern culture of comparison with norms. Either way Christians are caught in a 'paradigm of evaluation' (see Alexander 2007) all too clearly evocative of the Garden of Eden 'knowledge of good and evil'.

White (2000) explains the idea of living by society's norms:

> We have a culture of evaluation. These times could be called the 'grading times'…. When we trace the history of this culture of evaluation we can see how modern processes of the judgement of people's actions are intimately associated with, and in the service of, reproducing our society's constructed norms. Even just norms for living (p.110).

Because the West in general has left behind the black and white Right and Wrong of the religion of Christianity, we have chosen instead a comparison with constructed norms. There is a fascination for what is considered a norm – weight, education, income, development. We have rejected a hierarchy of authorities who used to check whether we were behaving correctly, but we have instead imposed upon ourselves the 'normalising gaze' – the self checking and comparison with the norms of our culture – "what will people think" has become a strong motivator in checking our behaviour, beliefs, attitudes and values.

While Christians have often thought they have rejected 'the world's' standards we have in fact absorbed this pernicious practice of evaluation. We just substitute what is considered 'normal' among Christians for what is considered normal by 'the world.', and then turn up the heat by calling these evaluations, all too often, spiritual, or godly, or 'biblical'. For example how many times a person goes to church, reads their Bible, what clothes they wear, what movies they watch, what books they read, which school their children attend – become subject to the 'normalising gaze' – that is, what is acceptable in the present culture of Western Christians - and the person is condemned for not coming up to the 'standards' of the 'Christian' culture. Christians, often more than their friends and neighbours, subject themselves to condemnation much more reminiscent of the Pharisees than of the Liberating Christ.

In fact the paradigm of evaluation leads to either self-condemnation or self-righteousness. As Christians have set up rules to live by, or 'Christian' norms to fit into, they have taken on the practices of the Pharisees - as Luke says it so graphically "certain people who were confident of their own goodness and looked down on others" (Luke 18: 9, Peterson). Jesus describes one of these, showing that his prayers demonstrate his own self-righteous stance: "O God, I do thank thee that I am not like the rest of mankind..." This was not "the one who went home 'justified'" – that is, knowing deeply his freedom, and finding relationship with God.

How ironic that the Man who challenged societal norms at every step is named as the founder of a religion which too often spawns implicit and explicit expectations more similar to 'the burdens tied on people's backs' as the Pharisees did. Paul despaired of even the early Christians in this regard: "Stand fast therefore in the liberty by which Christ has made us free, and do not be entangled again in the yoke of bondage" (Galatians 5:1 NIV). "Oh foolish Galatians. Who has bewitched you?... Having begun in the Spirit [life, freedom, relationship with God] are you now being made perfect by the flesh [striving, doing it Right]?" (Galatians 3: 1, 3). The most sorrowful part of all this is that we attribute to God this 'normalising gaze'. So many Christians, in their hearts, see God as always watching, checking, evaluating, to see if they are up to standard. The ultimate Critical Parent who can never be escaped.

In contrast Jesus was so often saying "Neither do I condemn you", and "It's your faith that's made you well." Jesus was looking for the person's own involvement in their growth, their own desire to get well or to change. He attributed growth to them personally, and undermined the authority of the religious structures and legalism which were so destructive. He lived out a transformative process in his interactions with those who came to him. He did this not by cutting across their way or directing them to change so much as calling forth 'the best' in them – the woman touching the edge of his garment, ashamed to speak to him was honoured as one whose faith saved her; Zaccheus the excluded tax collector became a generous

Christ-follower; Mary sitting at Jesus' feet was honoured as a disciple.

Many Christians today are learning to hear the gospel as good news, truth that brings freedom, rather than imbibing a religion which imposes external legalism and a Critical Policemen in the heavens. They are finding instead a God who stands with the oppressed and marginalised, who acknowledges their pain as well as their truth seeking and journey into abundant life.

The Narrative process hears the person's own story, aware of the places of suffering as indicators of values which have been overturned or not heard, seeking through these points the alternate story, the story of life, value, health and agency. It provides a means to companion this seeking of Reality, to highlight the choices for Life, and to honour the journey of each individual.

References

Alexander, I. (2007). *Dancing with God: Transformation through relationship.* London: SPCK.

Monk, G., Winslade, J., Crocket, K. & Epston, D. (1997). *Narrative therapy in practice: The archaeology of hope.* San Francisco: Jossey-Bass.

Morgan, A. (2000). *What is narrative therapy?* Adelaide: Dulwich.

White, M. (1995). *Re-authoring lives: Interviews and essays.* Adelaide: Dulwich.

White, M. (2000). *Reflections on narrative practice.* Adelaide: Dulwich.

White, M. (2002). Modern power and the production of failure. *The International Journal of Narrative Therapy and Community Work,* 3, 33-76.

White, M. (2003). Workshop in narrative therapy. Liverpool, England.

Chapter 8: Thinking beyond deficit positioning of self: Relevance for practice and faith

James Arkwright

About the author

Prior to 1993 I was engaged in farming and then rehabilitation following a spinal cord injury, at which time my career changed to counselling and then later counsellor education. I currently live in Tauranga, New Zealand with my wife and two children, where I teach counselling to student counsellors and am engaged in providing counselling and supervision.   Narrative ideas and practices have been informing this work for some years. Two major influences have been, firstly, my doctoral thesis, which focuses on researching the application of the concept of agency to the disability and illness experience, and secondly, training with Johnella Bird, Auckland. These have both significantly influenced how I understand the role of language and the operation of power relations in positioning people within the binary of either privilege or disadvantage. Further, they have enabled me to have increased understanding of the life of Jesus Christ and practical tools for continuing His work.

Introduction

Medical and psychological discourse works on the basis of assessing and treating for degrees of health and because of the dominance of this practice, especially within Western society, it has now become the norm for us to be judging how well in mind and spirit people are, including ourselves. Drawing from several writers within the soul care genre, I highlight critique of this practice which idealises the perfect self and the perfect life and then discusses how language can be re-configured so people can escape being positioned in such abject and deficit ways. Several examples of using an inquiry to re-position people so as to escape the binary of 'being OK or not' are provided, which then is briefly compared to Jesus Christ's way of relating to people, as portrayed in the Bible.

The deficit construction of self

> The configuration of the self, even a configuration composed of an absence, is socially constructed by those in power. The self is always a product of a specific cultural frame of reference, configured out of moral understandings and local politics. There are reasons and functions to most social phenomena, even if seemingly benign or obscure (Cushman, 1995, p.12).

Cushman made the above statement in his critique of modern psychotherapy, in which he details how the helping professions have constructed the self in deficit terms. His argument is that prevailing constructions of self in the Western world do not serve those who are most objectified by the construction; that is, those who are judged not mentally or emotionally well. A case in point is that all ten funding codes for New Zealand's Accident Compensation Commission's (ACC) sensitive claims (sexual abuse) counselling provision are diagnostic criteria found in the DSM IV (the Diagnostic and Statistical Manual of Psychiatric Disorders). Notably, only one of these codes, Post Traumatic Stress Disorder, contextualises a person's difficulties to their experiences within their social environment – as in 'this happened, which created these problematic effects', as opposed to 'the psychological difficulties relating to the intrinsic nature of a person's personality'.

Whilst all DSM IV diagnoses create a deficit, symptomatic and non-socially contexted account of the self, the personality disorders are arguably the most reductionist and pathologising of individuals. The following description of people diagnosed with borderline personality disorder, was described as a 'colorful account' by Davison and Neale (1994) in their abnormal psychology text:

The borderline patient is a therapist's nightmare....
They're the chronically depressed, the determinedly
addictive, the compulsively divorced, living from one
emotional disaster to the next. Bed hoppers, stomach
pumpers, freeway jumpers, and sad-eyed bench sitters
with arms stitched up like footballs and psychic
wounds that can never be sutured.... And they end up
taking temporary vacations in psychiatric wards and
prison cells, emerging looking good, raising everyone's
hopes, until the next let down, real or imagined, the
next excursion into self-damage. What they don't do is
change. (Kellerman, 1989, p. 113-114. In Davison &
Neale, 1994, p. 267-68)

It is hard to imagine a more pejorative description, nor how such a
positioning might in anyway be helpful for those people who are
viewed in such light.   Cushman's point is valid, psychological
discourse functions to separate clients from professionals,
positioning clients as not normal and problematic. Under some other
frame of reference it might be considered a crime to make a living
from assessing people in such abject ways. Moreover, I have heard
accounts of people (clients) who have felt shocked, re-abused and
even more gripped by desperation having read and signed their
ACC 'assessment for counselling report'.

The practice of naming or classifying a person's problem, whether it
be a formal psychological diagnosis or an informal labelling such as
'she manipulates' or 'he is selfish' are discursive interpretations and
unfortunately only too rarely are people's actual words and actions
explored so as to discover what they actually mean for them, and
further what social contexts have produced such talk and behaviour.
To some extent this practice of interpreting and positioning people in
absence of that which is desired may be a universal fault of the
human condition but there is some evidence that pastors during the
Renaissance prioritised an idea of 'caring for another's soul' in
comparison to today's psychological practice of assessing for the

degree of health. For example, the seventeenth century French pastor, François Félonelon, urged people to:

> Speak little; listen much; think far more of understanding hearts and adapting yourself to their needs than saying clever things to them. Show that you have an open mind, and let everyone see by experience that there is safety and consolation in opening his (sic) mind to you. (Félonelon, as cited in Benner, 1998, p.144)

Listening with an 'open mind', from a discursive point of view, could be taken to mean seeking to understand other people's thoughts, feelings and actions which are different from our own, no doubt having been shaped by different discourses than that which we have engaged with. When we do this, we are countering what Moore has termed "psychological modernism... that tends toward a mechanistic and rationalistic understanding of matters of the heart" (1994. p.206). In his view, current Western society first augments and then requires individuals to suppress and dislike psychological problems, such as depression:

> The 'bright' idea of colorizing old black and white movies is consistent with our culture's general rejection of the dark and gray. In a society that is defended against the tragic sense of life, depression will appear as an enemy, an unredeemable malady; yet in such a society, devoted to light, depression, in compensation, will be unusually strong. Some feelings and thoughts seem to emerge only in a dark mood. Suppress the mood, and you will suppress those ideas and reflections (Moore, 1994, p.138).

In a fast-paced Western consumerist culture that emphasises health and happiness as penultimate needs, people want quick answers and remedies to anything viewed as a personal problem. Moore, however, resists such requests, believing that the tragic aspects of life, and how they affect us, do have value:

> I don't try to eradicate problems... I try to give what is problematical back to the person in a way that shows its necessity, even its value. When people observe the ways in which the soul is manifesting itself, they are enriched, rather than impoverished. They receive back what is theirs, the very thing they have assumed to be so horrible that it should be cut out and tossed away. When you regard the soul with an open mind, you find the messages that lie within the illness, the corrections that can be found in remorse and other uncomfortable feelings, and the necessary changes requested by depression and anxiety (Moore, 1994, p. 5-6).

Moore echoes the shift of recent years to including spirituality in psychological health and therapy. Griffith and Griffith (2002) who are influenced by Narrative ideas specifically discuss the encounter with the sacred in psychotherapy. Kurtz and Ketcham have taken up a similar position to Moore in which they argue that the saints and sages of pre-Modernity "insist(ed) that imperfections be accepted as imperfections... endured and lived with creatively" (1992, p. 46). Such views, what might be termed a pre-Enlightenment form of spirituality or a soul care perspective, invite us to re-think how current Western society pursues the perfect life and the perfect self. Such an ideal leads to a comparison ethic, in which some people are viewed as healthier than others, less in deficit than others.

Deconstructing binary language descriptors

Any practice based on a comparison ethic operates on the notion that the presence of something, such as illness, is exclusive to its absence, that is, health. However, absence and presence are not exclusive but inter-dependant categories for one can only be known by way of the other (Burr, 1995). In this case, the division of health from illness does not make sense because both health and illness make up experience in that people simultaneously experience themselves as both well and not well, meaning that the invitations to be categorically defined as either well or ill can potentially be rejected.

Shifting from an understanding of people being either well or ill is an inherently political move because the either / or construction only serves the interest of those people who take up the privileged position within the binary. Moreover, the use of language that creates this mechanism of advantage is rarely negotiated or deconstructed. Bird (2004) explains:

> The politics I'm referring to relates to the way the conventional use of language works to generate a binary, i.e. either I am this or I am not this. When people who belong to marginalized groups consider the truth of a totalizing descriptor, they find limited belonging within this descriptor, e.g. 'Am I confident, ambitious, single-minded?' The descriptor which is readily available to them within the binary constructed world is an absence, e.g. 'I am not confident' or 'I am not determined'. Those people who are constructed within the presence, e.g. 'I am this,' believe this version of reality as 'true' and as solely an attribute of self. Conversely, those people who are constructed within an absence, e.g. 'I am not this,' also believe this version of reality as 'true' and consequently are drawn into interpreting and reinterpreting experiences which acts to confirm this deficit of self. I believe the use of conventional language obscures privilege while acting to colonise others at a profound level of identity (Bird, 2004, p.6).

As a person whose mobility is affected due to a spinal cord injury, I am very aware of how the either / or binary works in practice. For example, can I take my son to the beach and help him swim and have fun in the sea? The answer is 'no', and the answer to such 'can I do....' questions is often 'no' or 'not really' or 'only sometimes'. Hence, the dominant position available to me is one of absence, warranting conclusions such as 'I am limited as a Dad' or 'I can not be as good a Dad as men who do not have a spinal cord injury.' Unless those assumptions are deconstructed for what social frames of reference are informing such ideas then the view that I 'am a limited' parent or 'not as good a parent...' is unconsciously accepted as the truth. But if parenting competency is deconstructed through an exploration of the social contexts that have shaped such respective competencies and limitations, then a much broader and richer understanding of my parenting practices will be forthcoming, one that is more likely to position me as both competent and limited as a parent, as everyone is.

If language constructs the binary and is responsible for the construction of people in deficit, then it stands to reason that the use of language is critical for re-constructing the self so that it is not positioned in deficit. Bird (2000, 2004) discusses the process of using a relational inquiry for enabling this, which would aim, for example, to change the belief of myself as being limited as a Dad to the relationship between myself as a father and the idea of limitation.

Once I have been positioned in relation to 'the experience of limitation', a number of lines of inquiry can be explored, such as:
1. What are the ideas, practices, experiences of feelings and the body (Bird, 2004, p.45) that contribute to and make-up the experience of limitation, and its inverse - competency?
2. What social contexts have produced these particular ideas, practices, experiences of feelings and the body?
3. How have these particular ideas, practices, experiences of feelings and the body changed over time? (Bird, 2004, p.45)
4. What effects have these particular ideas, practices, experiences of feelings and the body had on my identity, actions and relationships?

The above exploration will inevitably be linked to wider social stories learned within family, schooling, community, work, other relationships and media. The success of the inquiry for seeing myself in relation to the experience of limitation and competency depends on having detailed and specific lines of inquiry which create multiple, rather than singular, descriptions of limitation and competency, such as: limitation at the beach, playing with a ball, dressing babies, helping children learn to swim and play sport, but competency in creating opportunities, being available, reading, listening, creating trust and fun, giving great wheelchair rides, being resourceful, a supporting partner and relating well to other parents.

The differentiation within and between kinds of limitation and competency makes it clear that the self need not be limited to the binary construction of either limitation or competency but can be reconfigured to become metaphoric categories of many types of both limitation and competency (Bird, 2004, p.68). Interestingly, the limitations only relate to physical tasks, conversely the competencies relate to mental and emotional skills, indicating the privileging of the idea that men must be physical whereas women will possess relational and emotional skills as parents.

The concept and practice of agency

Undertaking conscious choices about how to position oneself in relation to ideas, practices and experiences is often referred to as having agency or authority as it involves constructing new narrative responses to pejorative positioning. Bird (2004) has argued that a relational inquiry positions people to see the degree by which they are consciously active and choosing the social construction that has created the idea, feeling or practice they are experiencing. In illustrating a relational inquiry, I have chosen a fictional example of a conversation, with myself as the focus, which researches my experience of competency and deconstructs the social contexts that support this experience.

A: In contrast to these experiences of limitations, what experiences of competency do you have in the way you relate to and parent your children?

B: Ah, I guess, I'm quite a good listener.

A: As you consider this 'good listening competency', what words and feelings come forward?

B: Probably a few things, such as I do stop what I'm doing and listen when they're saying something to me… but I think lots of people do that.. I think the big thing, is that I listen for what is not being said.

A: When you are listening for what is not being said, what kinds of things do you notice?'

B: Oh, I notice the way they say things and I notice their emotions… and I guess I start wondering what else this might be about, other than what they're saying or how they're acting.

A: As you notice this what is not being said, how do you respond to it?

B: I try and stop myself saying what I'm about to say and ask a question.. like yesterday Caleb (toddler son) suddenly began to have a tantrum and rather than think, right, I've had enough of this and warn him to stop or else there will be consequences… I noticed where he was looking – at another cup, not the one I was giving him – and I said do you want your milk in that cup?' to which he said 'yes' – tantrum over.

A: What difference do you think this noticing what is not being said and then asking a question, makes for Caleb?

B: Oh, I think it helps him feel understood.

A: When Caleb feels understood, how do you imagine it effects the kind of boy he is growing into and the kind of relationship he has with you?

B: Well, I can't know for sure but I'd like to think it helps him feel secure in himself and secure in his relationship with me.

The relational inquiry has been effective for reconstructing my-self from being in deficit because a relationship with the experience of competence has been engaged with.   Moreover, the listening competency has been researched in light of how I am active in its construction and what differences it makes. The relational language positions my-self in relation to the idea of having a good listening competency', which becomes the practice of 'noticing what is not being said', that in turn produces the effects of Caleb feeling understood, secure in his relationship with himself and others.

As well as researching my relationship with the presence of competency, a relational inquiry might also explore how the contextual environment impacts on my ability to have a relationship with 'listening competency':

A: I'm just wondering, are there some times when this practice of noticing what is not being said, happens more or less than other times?

B: Yeah, I'd say so.

A: Do you have any ideas about what might bring this noticing practice forward in your relating with your children, or what might push it further into the background?

B: I think ideas about needing to get on top of problem behaviour pushes it into the background.

A: When are those ideas most present?

B: When we've been watching one of those super nanny programmes.. you know the ones, when the nanny says – wagging her finger – you've been a very very naughty boy! (laughs)… or when we've had (a person) come to stay, who always seems to judging the way we're raising our kids.

A: How do those experiences stop you noticing what is not being said?

B: I think I have to be this big parent who is in charge of the kids and I start wondering if I'm not tough enough and then I forget to just be in the moment with the kids.

A: Are you saying that being in the moment stands behind this practice of noticing what is not being said'?

B: Yes, I think so.

A: Can you reflect for a moment, on what have been the times and ways that you have stepped into this being in the moment? How has this practice of being in the moment worked in your life and what and who has supported it?

The practice of noticing what is not being said is re-searched in relation to the contextual environment that impacts it, as in what has brought forward the respective ideas and practices that both limit and strengthen my relationship with the noticing of what is not being said. When I do this, I am using relational language which positions me to make meaning of and reflect on experience quite differently from when using conventional language:

Relational Language-Making	Conventional Language-Use
The experience of limitation	I am limited or I'm not limited
The type of parenting I practice, use or engage with	I am a good parent or I am not a good parent
The listening ability I use with my son	I am a good listener or I am not a good listener
The practice of noticing what is said and what is not said	I attend well or I don't attend well

John

Below is a summary of my conversations with John in which I endeavoured to use relational language, develop multiple language descriptions, explore new positions for John to take-up in regard to the problem of procrastination so he could experience being less positioned in deficit and have an increased sense of agency in his life.

John told me how he had been reflecting on the problem of procrastination in his life. He said that for the 2 ½ years that he had been doing his degree and during his years at secondary school, he had always viewed himself as having problems with school (academic) work. He knew he procrastinated when it came to doing assignments, with the result he often handed in assignments late and missed lectures because he was working frantically to get an assignment completed by the due time. The result was that he felt bad about himself and knew that others also regarded him as having a problem with managing his time and getting work in on time. He was being positioned in the absence of being a good student.

It had occurred to John that within the academic environment a lot of priority was given to written work. He usually got good marks but was quite often penalised for not handing work in on time. He started questioning this practice of privileging written work produced within a time-frame set by the lecturers, and he wondered how well this practice fairly measured what people knew and understood of a topic. He also concluded that although he didn't mind the writing aspect of assignments, the part he really enjoyed was the reading for assignments (he read copiously for each assignment). We then started to be curious together as to how this inequality between what is valued as creditable knowledge could be re-storied. I asked John if we might think of it as different types of learning, of which writing learning was only one way in which to learn and prove competency on knowing a subject. John and I then thought about the kinds of ways that he learned and we named them: reading learning, thinking learning, writing learning and conversation learning. These metaphoric categories gave John a different set of measures by which to view his relationship with learning. For example, he may have invested much time in thinking, reading and conversation learning for a particular assignment but spent less time in writing learning. However, within academic discourse there was no recognition of the thinking, reading and conversation learning he had undertaken.

I asked John, if he had any ideas on how God might view the learning he did when doing an assignment. John replied that God knew what was done in secret so He would see all the different ways he learned but that God would be interested in the attitude and heart a person had toward their learning; were they doing their learning (work) unto the Lord. This gave John a way of seeing his progress with learning which whilst it recognized the consequences of not meeting the requirements of academic discourse, he could still view himself as having applied himself as a student in his learning. John found it very liberating to think of his learning in this way, which counteracted the story of him being a 'slack student'.

In a later conversation John and I explored how he had taken up the practice of putting-off the 'writing learning' aspect of learning. He remembered some incidences in school, in which a teacher's response to him meant that he lived in fear of being criticized for his schoolwork and as a refuge he spent time in the library and at home reading. He came to love reading. We discussed how he could transfer his confidence, love and skill in reading to the task of writing. John did still struggle at times with handing in work on time but not to the point where he was asked to re-do papers the following year. He also saw himself in a new light, one that helped him understand how and why he had developed the learning practices of reading learning, thinking learning and conversation learning. This new understanding enabled John to stand up to the label of being a slack student, which helped him both work harder at his 'writing learning' whilst appreciating his diligence at the other forms of learning. In short, John was no longer positioned in the absence of being a good student. He was firmly putting behind him the ADHD diagnosis he had been given at high school.

Again, the process of relational language positions people to understand their experience and themselves quite differently, less in-deficit terms, than when conventional language is used:

Relational Language-Making	Conventional Language-Use
The engagement with reading, thinking and conversation in learning	I procrastinate
The prioritization of reading, thinking and conversation in learning	I'm not a good student
The attitude and heart I bring to learning is important	I have ADHD
The fear of criticism	I'm frightened of criticism

The agenda of agency relating to aspects of Jesus' ministry

A relational inquiry was helpful for John escaping being constructed in deficit. The development of the metaphoric categories of 'learning' for John enabled him to avoid the either / or categories of binary logic, in which he had taken up a position in the absence of how he should be as a student and indirectly speaking, as a person as well. The result of undertaking a relational enquiry was that John was better able to appreciate what he did well – the reading, thinking and conversation learning, none of which were being acknowledged adequately, and he was more able to focus on improving his writing learning thereby discrediting the label of slack student and diagnosis of ADHD.

When I think about John no longer being positioned in such deficit terms, it reminds me of how I perceive Jesus related to people. When the woman was caught in adultery (John 8:3-11) Jesus responded in a way that positioned her as having sin in her life just like everyone else and because no one was 'without sin' she was not stoned to death and Jesus said he did not condemn her either. When Jesus' disciples rebuked and sent away the children who were brought to Him, Jesus re-positioned the children in regard to their status in society, saying 'let the little children come to me, and do not hinder them, for the kingdom of heaven belongs to such as these' (Matthew 19:13-15). Similarly, Jesus did not reject and discriminate against the Samaritan women at the well (which was normal cultural practice for a Jew) but instead talked with her and received water from her, which was so impacting on her that she went back to the village saying 'Come see a man who knew all about the things I did, who knows me inside and out' (John 4:1-30). Clearly, she felt understood and accepted by Jesus. When Simon the Pharisee was disapproving of the woman pouring expensive perfume on Jesus' feet and washing them with her hair he did not reject her but instead rejected Simon's criticism of her. Jesus praised her for the way she had welcomed and cared for him (Luke 7: 36-50).

In fact, the more that people were positioned in absence, the more Jesus seemed to both accept them and find something to acknowledge and appreciate about them. He found another description for their life, one that positioned them less in absence which, as a consequence, changed who they were and what they did. For example, Zacchaeus, the chief tax collector who could only see Jesus by climbing up a tree, was first acknowledged by Jesus and then Jesus invited himself back to Zacchaeus' house for lunch, an action that overrode how Jews would normally think about and relate to tax collectors. The impact of this re-positioning on Zacheuss was that he said "and now I give half of my possessions to the poor, and if I have cheated anybody out of anything, I will pay back four times the amount" (Luke 19:1-10).

However, not only did Jesus' actions re-position people so they were less in deficit, the stories he told did the same as well. The parable of the Good Samaritan illustrated the imperative of seeing past cultural bias, instead understanding and meeting a person's need (Luke 10:29-37). In contrast, when discourse was positioning people in privilege, but the advantage created by that positioning was used to oppress and discriminate, then Jesus attacked that privileging and abuse of power, such as when he said, 'Woe to you, teachers of the law and Pharisees, you hypocrites! You are like whitewashed tombs, which look beautiful on the outside but on the inside are full of dead men's bones and everything unclean. In the same way, on the outside you appear to people as righteous but on the inside you are full of hypocrisy and wickedness' (Matthew 23:13-33). In doing this, Jesus gave voice to another description, one that undermined the positioning of privilege and power accorded to the Jewish leaders.

Conclusion

As I read the Gospel accounts of Jesus it seems clear to me that Jesus re-positioned people who were viewed in deficit. In following Christ's model for living it seems important that I need to be doing the same, but the configuration of binaries within language descriptions means it is not always easy to do this. Bird explains that when she says that those constructed within either the presence or absence of desired personality traits believe the reality of that version to be true (2004, p.6). It is my hope that this discussion about using relational language and finding multiple accounts to escape singular binary descriptions may help people re-position themselves less in deficit and experience more agency in their lives, for I believe that this is a practice that resonates with and can give witness to the life of Christ.

References

Arkwright, J. (2005). Disability: Theorising experiences in the critical analysis of discourse. *New Zealand Journal of Disability Studies*, 33-56.

Benner, D. (1998). *Care of souls: Revisioning Christian nurture and counsel.* Grand Rapids: Baker Books.

Bird, J. (2000). *The heart's narrative: Therapy and navigating life's contradictions.* Auckland: Edge Press.

Bird, J. (2004). *Talk that sings: Therapy in a new linguistic key.* Auckland: Edge Press.

Burr, V. (1995). *An introduction to social constructionism.* New York: Routledge.

Cushman, P. (1995). *Constructing the self, constructing America.* Reading, MA: Addison-Wesley.

Davison, G. & Neale, J. (1994). *Abnormal psychology. (6ᵗʰ edn.).* New York: John Wiley & Sons.

Griffith, J. & Griffith, M. (1992). Owning one's own epistemological stance in therapy. *Dulwich Centre Newsletter, (1),* 5-11.

Kurtz, E., & Ketcham, K. (1992). *The spirituality of imperfection: Storytelling and the search for meaning.* New York: Bantam

Moore, T. (1994). *Care of the soul: A guide for cultivating depth and sacredness in everyday life.* New York: HarperPerennial.

Parker, I. & Shotter, J. (1990). (Eds.). *Deconstructing social psychology.* London: Routledge.

Sampson, E. (1989). The deconstruction of self. In J. Shotter & K. Gergen. (Eds.). *Texts of identity.* (pp.1-17). London: Sage.

Shotter, J. & Gergen, K. (1989). (Eds.). *Texts of identity.* London: Sage.

White, M. (2001). Personal agency and intentional states. *International Journal of Narrative Therapy and Community Work (2),* 18-25.

SECTION TWO: CHRISTIANS PUTTING NARRATIVE IDEAS INTO PRACTICE

Chapter 9: The Self God knows and the socially constructed identity

Donald McMenamin

About the author

My name is Donald McMenamin. I live in Auckland, New Zealand. I work half time as a counsellor in a local High School, and half time in private practice. In private practice I see people for counselling and supervision, and teach in the counsellor education programme at The Bible College of New Zealand.

Introduction

Identity is often viewed as the essential self within a person. This chapter presents a view of the Self as something God created. Identity is then defined as the discovery of the God-created Self as a person relates with the social world. Narrative Therapy is then presented as an effective means of helping persons to make sense of their experience and identify aspects of their God-created Self in order to live this Self more fully and more congruently in the world.

The Self

You turned my wailing into dancing; you removed my sackcloth and clothed me with joy, that my heart may sing to you and not be silent. O LORD my God, I will give you thanks forever (Psalm 30:11-12).

Imagine a world where the nature of a person's self is measured by the actions they take. And imagine in this world that every possible action has a standard, and the value of a person's self is measured against that standard. And imagine that, from birth, everyone in this world is trained to evaluate themselves and others according to these standards, making decisions about whether or not they and others are 'good' selves. In this imaginary world people value the skill of judging others. People become adept at imposing standards on others, and looking as though they are meeting set standards themselves (White, 1995; White & Denborough, 2005).

Imagine a second world, where people are known according to their intentions. In this imaginary world the nature of a person's self is seen in what they intend by their actions, what they are aiming for in their actions, what they are standing for and hoping for in their actions. And imagine that, from birth, everyone in this world is trained to be curious about what people are aiming for in their actions so as to see what it is they are standing for in acting that particular way. In this imaginary world people value the skill of curiosity. People become adept at asking and answering questions about what they consider important in life (White, 2001).

Imagine that God created a person as an eternal Self to live in one of these worlds. In which of these worlds, do you think, that eternal Self would be more likely to thrive?

Aligning identity (who am I?) and the God-known Self

All a man's ways seem right to him, but the LORD weighs the heart (Proverbs 21:2).

My interest in Narrative ideas stems from when I first read a counselling article by Michael White. This article put into words things that I had been feeling but had no language for: respect for people and that people are not their problems. This sat well with me. The idea that there is always another account of a person's actions was important.

Later I took the chance to study Narrative Therapy at the University of Waikato. That first interest grew into enthusiasm for and an on-going practice in Narrative Therapy. Since then I have worked as a counsellor in several New Zealand high schools, mainly with teenage students. I have developed a practice of supervision with other counsellors and taken up positions teaching counselling, both in organisations and in private practice.

When I first encountered Narrative ideas they resonated with my own understandings of helpful ways to be with people. At the same time I understand there have been misgivings among parts of the Christian community about the effects of post modern/social constructionist ideas, which form part of Narrative Therapy's thinking. This led me to ask, "What place do ideas of the social construction of identity as expressed in Narrative Therapy have in the life of a person committed to searching out and living in what they understand as God's ways? Can an understanding of Identity as socially constructed assist at all in this project?"

First it would be useful to look at what I am meaning when I use the words 'Self' and 'Identity'. I see the Self as being a self-in-relationship-with-God. When I imagine my self-in-relationship-with-God, what I see in my mind is a scene: I approach Jesus – He is a man like me, warm faced and pleased to see me. There are many people watching, with a sprit of anticipation among them as if they are about to see something funny, something to be enjoyed. As I approach Jesus, mindful of all He has made possible for me, I bow at the waist. And He, serious, bows equally to me. I bow even lower, and He, with a glint of laughter in His eye, bows lower too! I sense a game of fun, and prostrate myself before Him. He, laughing, flips onto His head and twirls about. I copy that and we laugh, full-chested laughs. Then all the people laugh, delighted, and we dance together. He and I. All of us together.

When I think of my Self-in-relationship-with-God, it is this unexpected joyous dance that I imagine. An always-will-be dance (Lewis, 1943). I have used the phrase God-known Self here, because although the dance is of equals, it is at His initiation that we are equals. It is His knowing of me that causes the dance to be. This is my sense of my Self-in-relationship-with-God, or my God-known Self.

However, it seems that, sometimes in everyday life I forget this dance that is my God-known Self. I get distanced from the knowledge of the Relationship that both creates and sustains me.

My 'Identity' differs from my God-known Self in that my Identity is the result of the everyday conclusions I arrive at when I think about who I am. It seems that I have a constant struggle to keep in touch with my awareness of my God-known Self, my Self-in-eternal-relationship-with-God. I find all too frequently in my everyday life that I am thinking of myself as unloved, of little value or without purpose. These Identity conclusions stand in marked contrast to what at times I know of my Self-in-relationship-with-God. In those times of remembering I know myself to be 'a beloved son', invited to 'abide in Him,' a source of joy and fun for Him and for others. My everyday Identity is often at odds with my (for the moment forgotten) God-known Self.

I understand it to be part of my life's purpose to be as aware as possible in my everyday life of the reality of who-I-am-in-God. That is to say, to align my everyday Identity (who I am) with the truth (the dance) of my God-known Self.

The basis of this chapter is that the practices of Narrative Therapy provide useful tools in the project of remembering the nature of my Self-in-relationship, my God-known Self; and that in remembering, I can express a self in keeping with that knowledge. The value of Narrative Therapy is that it provides practices to explore, remember, and make choices about the way I describe my Self. It places me more clearly as an author of my Identity, aligning 'Who I am' with a mindful awareness of my Self-in-relationship-with-God; speaking about myself with a growing awareness of that eternal reality.

A word about the politics of language

All language is arrived at in an on-going process of assigning agreed meanings to given words, actions, and events. In this way all language is located within the culture of the people who agree to those meanings. This process of assigning meaning to words, actions and events is political. It is political in that it reflects the culture within which it takes place, and it reflects the power relations within that culture. Of the different versions possible for the meaning of an event or an experience, it is one version that is adopted and not others. Which are actually dominant is a political process.

The process of arriving at meanings, and agreeing to them, has an effect of excluding, or relegating to the fringe, alternative and competing possibilities for meaning. In this way commonly agreed meanings may obscure other alternative meanings. Whose meanings end up being the commonly agreed meanings for an experience or event is a political process, the result of competition for meaning-making (Monk, Winslade, Crocket and Epston, 1997; White, 1995). Over time, given meanings for experience and events become widely accepted as true, and in this way become dominant, and seem self-evidently true.

Narrative Therapy uses the term discourse to describe these socially agreed, seemingly self-evidently 'true' meanings. Over time these dominant discourses take up the position of seeming not only right, but self-evidently so. Other ways of making meaning can be seen as of lesser or fringe value, or simply wrong.

What has this to do with identity?

As soon as language is introduced to our understanding of our God-known Self, this political process of taken-for-granted meaning making begins. Whose version of reality is adopted and whose is not, who benefits from these conclusions and who does not, who is positioned as powerful and who is not – is largely unquestioned. Alternative possibilities for meaning-making of knowledge and experience of Self are overlooked and left unexplored. In this way preferred versions of the meaning of experience can be overlooked in favour of socially dominant, seemingly self-evident, 'true' meanings of experience.

This leads to the possibility, even likelihood, that people's Identity, the meaning people make of their everyday experience of Self, are a product of a taken-for-granted process, rather than a result of carefully chosen, experience-near consideration. In this sense the Identity can be seen as largely socially constructed.

If our interest lies in our expression of Self being as closely aligned with our understanding and experience of our God-known Self as possible then processes such as Narrative Therapy which invite thinking carefully about meaning-making, exposing the politics of meaning making, and the careful consideration of alternatives to standard meanings, will serve this interest well.

It is worth asking here, 'Why am I interested in aligning my everyday Identity with my God-known Self?' For me the answer is simple. When I remember who-I-am-in-God, when I reconnect with that Relationship within which I have my being, I experience peace and purpose. I remember I am conceived and sustained in Love. The words, 'You are my beloved son' and the invitation 'Abide in Me' create a sense of well-being that has me at ease within my Self. In turn that well-being empowers me to act in the world in ways in keeping with my God-known Self.

In contrast, when I forget who I am, when I am distanced from my awareness of that sustaining Relationship, I am often sad, lonely, bewildered – I like and enjoy myself less, and lose vision and purpose for my life. The more I have my everyday understanding of my self, my Identity, in line with my eternal Self-in-relationship-with-God, the better off I am. At the heart of Narrative Therapy is an ability to reflect on how I make meaning of life, and an opportunity to make choices about the Identity conclusions that flow from the meanings I make.

The importance of all this is that, in looking more carefully into which of my multitude of experiences I will use to speak about my Identity, and which of the competing meanings for those experiences I will adopt, I can make clearer choices about my Identity in ways that align more closely with my growing understanding of my God-known Self. Narrative Therapy aids this process through a series of practices that can be termed conversation maps (White & Denborough, 2005; White, 2007).

In a conversation map the direction of interest of both counsellor and client, and the questions that support that interest, are described. The metaphor of a map is useful because the conversation so described is not linear and may range about the territory of the map, while remaining within its overall view.

Conversation maps can help to expose the effects of taken-for-granted interpretations of life, provide a chance to take a position for or against those effects, and to clarify why one might take that position. This provides an opportunity for the values of the Self-in-God to come to the fore. Where the effects of everyday interpretations of life are not in keeping with the values of the God-known Self, and where one chooses to act differently in keeping with those God-known Self values, Narrative Therapy provides an invitation to repentance – a turning towards the preferred.

Conversation maps also draw connections between the preferred interpretations, and the people who stand together in those interpretations. These maps provide opportunities to invite these valued others to respond to preferred Identity claims, and to speak about the effect of those claims in their own lives, building further experiences of life in relationship.

The conversation maps of Narrative Therapy provide support in making preferred claims about Identity, claims that align Identity with the values and purposes of the God-known Self. These maps also provide structures or scaffolds within which those preferred claims of identity can be explored and developed, and in which communities of support for preferred identity claims can be developed.

Statement of Position maps

These maps have been fully described elsewhere (Winslade & Monk, 1999; Morgan, 2000; White & Epston, 1990; Freedman & Combs, 1996; Monk et al, 1997; White, 2007). This section will show how I have utilised them in working with young people.

Mapping Externalising Conversations

This map outlines a conversation within which a problem experienced by a person is named in ways that fit with their experience of it. The problem is spoken of as external to the person. The effects of this problem in the life of the person and others are closely explored across a range of situations and times. The person is invited to take up a position about the problem and its effects – "how does all this fit with the person you prefer to be?" The conversation goes on to explore why it is that the person has taken up that position and what that suggests about their commitments and purposes in life.

The example below is a letter in which the effects of the problem are explored and the responses of the person are made clear (White & Epston, 1990). It is these responses which show the preferred identity, the person's Self-in-relationship-with-God. For Harry below, the identification of kindness is a hint of his God-known self that we discover in our work together:

Dear Harry,
Thanks for the conversation today. Working with you as a detective is fun for me! (Brown coats, bowler hats, flash cars...)
My understanding is that you and your family have been suffering for the crimes of a very sneaky Problem.

The crimes perpetrated against you and your family include:

- Making you miss dinners
- Having you take time off school
- Producing sicknesses in you from its bag of illnesses
- Making key people think that you are at fault (problems often make other people take the blame)
- Sometimes this Problem has you thinking you are not a very worthy person to be around
- Sometimes it gets you upset and angry (even occasionally in a 'blind rage'.)
- Stealing up to 30% of your academic potential
- Threatening terrible future crimes of damaging your future relationships, children, job prospects
- Whispering sad thoughts like "Its much better to stop home today" and "Stay home"

Together we were able also to uncover an accomplice in the form of PS2 which can join this Problem in whispering "Play me!" And, not surprisingly given the range of tricks and mates this Problem has got, you have sometimes been tricked into cooperating with its plans! No worries. Today is a new day!

And you have resisted it – yes?
- Every single mufti day you resisted it.
- On normal days, especially when Japanese is on first or last, you resisted it.
YOU HAVE THE POWER!!

Anyway, Harry, we talked last about you being a KIND guy. Not a sap sort of kind (but sap is good for trees) but a strength/kindness sort of guy. And maybe that will help us in this quest we have to kick this Problem out of your life? We'll see.

Harry, I'm looking forward to the next instalment… Until then, keep a note of any Resistance that you notice, and I'll see you soon.

All the very best
Mr Mac.

In this example the Problem and its tactics have been exposed, and Harry has taken the opportunity to stand against the Problem and its effects. That he chooses to do so, and the direction he chooses to move in, is an articulation of the nature of his God-known-Self.

Mapping Re-authoring Conversations

People make sense of their lives by connecting experiences or events in their life across time according to some theme or plot - hence the term: Narrative Therapy (Epston, 1989; White, 1995; Russell & Carey, 2004; White, 2007). Re-authoring conversations invite people to do just this. They focus on forgotten or neglected experiences or responses from the person's life. Regardless of how a person's life has been storied, there will always be actions, intentions, hopes and possibilities that have existed which have not been included in the dominant account of their life. Re-authoring conversations are interested in recalling these un-included examples of experience so that a person has them available for alternative meaning-making of their life and experience.

In Re-authoring conversations the process of questioning assists people to recall and link forgotten or overlooked experience in their life. This process has two areas of enquiry:
- The actions and experiences of a person's life, and
- The identity conclusions drawn from those actions and experiences.

In re-engaging with their own life history, people experience an opportunity to draw alternative Identity conclusions. From this perspective it is possible for people to begin to speculate as to what they might want to do in the future. These future steps are seen in the light of the person's purposes in life, their hopes and dreams for themselves and others, and their commitments in life.

This process of a re-authoring conversation invites a person to revisit their experience of life and put together formerly forgotten or overlooked experiences into an account of what is important for them in life. This account includes what they are choosing to stand for in life leading to Identity conclusions that fit more closely with their preferred values and commitments in life. This is an example of the effect of the second world referred to in the introduction to this chapter, a world where the focus is on intention rather than behaviour alone. Focussing on actions as evidence of intentions and commitments provides a powerful antidote to the taken for granted and dominant meaning making that may have previously informed a sense of Identity.

The following document shows an example of a re-authored life account. Here the preferred account of life is made public and celebrated (White, 1995):

Dear Mrs. Tapa,

Over the past couple of weeks I have had the chance to meet with your daughter, Tania, and to hear something of her story. As we have talked it seemed to us that Tania has made real progress in moving from one sort of lifestyle to another, so we decided to try and record what she has done so that others could know that to!

As a result, may I send you this Certificate? Tania and I have written it together. It has been a pleasure to meet with your daughter. Her gentle maturity impressed me. Please contact me if I can help in any way.

Warmly
Donald McMenamin

**This certificate is to record the Effort and Achievement made
by**

Tania Tapa

in her journey away from violence as a way of life
and towards peace and maturity as a way of life.

When Tania realised (after some years) that Violence is not the key, she resolved to make a move to stop violence. To achieve this Tania has:

- Moved country
- Prayed daily
- Cooled herself when anger was near
- Tried not to think about it
- Recognised that violence is a childish way
- Made a commitment to move towards maturity and wisdom
- Recognised some of God's plan for her life
- Known that 'When something bad happens, something good comes at the end."

The success of Tania's efforts at school have been recognised by **ALL** her teachers. Tania said: **"The whole report was GOOD!"**
At times Tania has wanted to give up this journey towards maturity and peace. At those times these things have helped:

- Thinking long term
- Wondering 'What will the outcome be?'
- Having someone to lift her up – to support her
- Knowing that it will be better.

This journey that Tania is on leads to starting again, to non-violence, to maturity and living a helping life.

**This Certificate is to recognise Tania Tapa
and her effort and commitment in her journey
towards Peace and Maturity.**

Signed: Mr Donald McMenamin
Official recorder of Excellent Efforts.

In this example the re-authored accounts of Identity are made clearer for Tania and for her audience, people who care about her. Much of the detail of these stories had been either forgotten, or considered unimportant. The actions described here had not previously been assembled as a coherent account of what this person stands for in life. Implicit within this account is evidence for the nature of Tania's Self-in-God – her choices of moving from one lifestyle to another and the steps she took along the way. In making this explicit and public, stories like this support the person in their goal of living out this preferred account of the Self.

Mapping Re-membering Conversations

Relationships with significant others are important in the pursuit and maintenance of preferred Identity conclusions. Claims that are in keeping with a person's knowledge and experience of their God-known Self are supported and strengthened when they are joined with significant others (Russell & Carey, 2004; Morgan, 2000; White, 2007).

Reviewing a person's relationships over time may remind people of others who have been significant in some way in this emerging alternative account of their life and Identity. These relationships, and the effects of them in supporting Identity claims, can be further explored in a re-membering conversation.

The re-membering conversation begins with a rich account of the way that this significant person contributed to the person's life. This is followed by an invitation for the person to view themselves through the eyes of this significant other, and to explore their preferred Identity conclusions through the eyes of the other.

This looking at one's Identity through the eyes of the other is followed by an exploration of the ways that the person has contributed to the life of the significant other. The re-membering conversation continues with an invitation to explore the effects of these contributions on the significant other's life and identity.

This process richly describes the relationships of the person with significant others, and explores the effects of those relationships on both parties. In this way the Identity conclusions that are being explored are more fully located in the context of important relationships, and the effects of those relationships are made transparent.

In the example below, a letter was sent to a community of care inviting them to respond with accounts of the person, as they know them. These wider accounts stand both as an antidote to problem accounts and they serve to establish and strengthen a community of care and relationship around the person.

The responses from the community become another resource from which a person can select in building an Identity that is in keeping with their sense of Self. This is just the beginning of the process described above.

TO WHOM IT MAY CONCERN
RE: PATTI STEVENS

After consulting widely among school staff, family relations and friends, we have been able to compile a list of qualities and abilities that goes some way towards describing
PATTI STEVENS
as she is seen by others who know her well. Descriptions like these can never be complete and while older qualities continue to develop, newer qualities are quietly being added.
Nonetheless this Certificate aims to attempt one possible description of
PATTI STEVENS
When asked, people who know PATTI well offered these descriptions...

RESPONSIBLE
Carries responsibility through well, contributes to what's going on, self-motivated, works very well, and accepts responsibility.

FUN TO BE AROUND
Makes work fun, sense of humour, gets along with everyone, friendly, easy-going, open loving disposition, enthusiastic.

HELPS OTHERS
Humour that helps others, understands well, liked by others, good talker, helps friends, welcoming.

MATURE
Assertive, confident, sensible, accepts when things go wrong, positively argumentative, makes good points, perseverance, mature, honest, integrity, leadership.

These people also made it clear that PATTI has demonstrated a commitment to and achievement in
Photography, Swimming, Netball, Skiing, Cooking, Sewing, Singing, Maths, and Computers.
This Certificate is Delighted to AFFIRM and ACKNOWLEDGE the on-going development and achievements of
PATTI STEVENS

Signed
D. McMenamin
Editor-in-Chief
Preferred Personality Projects.

The community of care is reflecting what it is they see of the nature of the person which is the Self-in-relationship-with-God. In using these responses as a resource, the person is assisted in aligning their Identity with their God-known self. What is not recorded here is an exploration of the effects on the community of describing the person in this way. Exploring ways that the person has affected the lives of others, and exploring how those effects have contributed to the community's identity adds richly to the story the person holds about themselves.

Outsider Witness practices

As people develop a sense of Identity that is in keeping with their experience of their God-known Self, they make claims about their Identity – "this is who I am and what I stand for." These claims can be supported and strengthened by inviting a group to be witnesses to the Identity claims being made. This process is called Outsider Witness practices. Re-membering conversations, as above, can easily be part of Outsider Witness practices (White, 1995;Russell & Carey, 2004; Morgan, 2000; Freedman & Combs, 1996; White, 2007).

In this practice a person is invited to give an account of their experience and the Identity claims that arise from this. This account is listened to by the Outsider Witness group who are invited to respond in particular ways with a re-telling of the account they have heard. This re-telling is listened to by the person who, in turn, is invited to re-tell their hearing of the outsider witness' account.

These processes of telling and re-telling are guided by four categories of response:
1.   Identifying the expression: What caught your attention? What words and phrases stood out for you? What struck you?
2.   Describing the image: What does this suggest to you about what is important to this person? What does this suggest they are standing for in life? What image or metaphor comes to mind as you think about this?

3.   Resonating responses: How does what stood out for you connect with your own life? Can you tell a story that helps us understand why that stood out for you?

4.   Acknowledging transport: How has listening and responding in these ways shifted you? As a result of this conversation are you changed in any way? Does being a part of this suggest anything for your own next steps?

Outsider Witness tellings not only support and encourage the preferred Identity claims being made, they also add richly to the account of them, and to the account of the effect of those claims in the lives of others.

Below is an example of an invitation to a meeting where these tellings and re-tellings will be held. In these tellings and re-tellings a rich account of people's perception of the person's Identity is put forward. This can strongly support the person's preferred claims about their Identity, and build connections between Selves in community and the Community of people-in-God.

To the People who Believe
in Graham Bart's Ability to Control Behaviour

Lately there has been a story around that Graham's behaviour is out of Graham's control. This story says that Graham requires medication to stay in control. Graham and I believe that there are many people who do not agree with the description that Graham's behaviour is out of his control. Graham and I believe there are a number of people who know that Graham has controlled his behaviour in the past, can do so now, and will do so in the future.

Graham names some of these people as Mum, Dad, Richard, Annette, Katee, Mr Tread, Mr Splice, Mr Sorenson, and Mr McMenamin. Graham says that having a group of people who believe in his ability to control his own behaviours helps to provide him with the strength and resolve to carry out this task. He does not say it is easy. He does say he can do it.

Graham and I invite you as the people who believe in Graham to a meeting to re-affirm to Graham that we believe in him and that we support his efforts to prove that he is in control of his own behaviours.

Graham affirms how important your belief in him is to him.

The meeting will be held on Friday 6th June at 1.20pm in the seminar room, B block corridor, Harbour High School. Guests will be met at the main office at 1.15pm. If for any reason this time is not available for you please contact Mr McMenamin.

Looking forward to meeting with you.

Warm regards
Graham Bart
Donald McMenamin

This kind of invitation positioned supportive others as witnesses to Graham's story of progress – his alternate story. The Outsider Witness process is another of the maps that can effectively structure and guide a narrative exploration.

Conclusion

Earlier I proposed two questions as
•   What place do ideas of the social construction of Identity have in the life of a person committed to searching out and living in what they understand as God's ways? and
•   Can an understanding of Identity as socially constructed as in Narrative Therapy assist at all in this project?

In making meaning of life we often assume that our actions are evidence of our internal nature. In contrast to this, I have proposed that Narrative Therapy helps us to see how our intentions in life speak more clearly about our God-known Self. This understanding liberates us to re-story our experience in line with what we stand for, and with what we are committed to in life, with the values of our God-known Self.

Narrative practices provide a forum within which a sense of Identity can be explored, and within which alternative and preferred claims about Identity can be made and witnessed by others.

This opportunity to reflect carefully on Identity conclusions, and to review the processes in which Identity claims have been made, is a powerful way to consult one's own sense of God-known Self, and to align Identity claims with that sense of Self.

In providing tools that assist in developing mindful and experience near Identity claims, Narrative Therapy supports the project of aligning everyday Identity with one's God-known Self.

In the words of the Psalmist "May the words of my mouth and the meditation of my heart be pleasing in your sight, O LORD, my Rock and my Redeemer" (Psalm 19:14).

References

Epston, D. (1989). *Collected papers*. Adelaide: Dulwich Centre.

Freedman, J. & Combs, G. (1996). *Narrative therapy*. New York: Norton.

Lewis, C. S. (1943). *Mere Christianity*. New York: MacMillan

Morgan, A. (2000). *What is narrative therapy?* Adelaide: Dulwich Centre

Monk, G., Winslade, J., Crocket, K. & Epston, D. (1997). *Narrative therapy in practice. The archaeology of hope*. San Francisco: Jossey-Bass.

Russell, S. & Carey, M. (2004). *Narrative therapy: Responding to your questions*. Adelaide: Dulwich Centre.

Winslade, J. & Monk, G. (1999). *Narrative counselling in schools.* Californina: Corwin Press.

White, C. & Denborough, D. (2005). *A community of ideas.* Adelaide: Dulwich Centre.

White, M. (1995). *Re-authoring lives: Interviews and essays.* Adelaide: Dulwich Centre.

White, M. & Epston, D. (1990). *Narrative means to therapeutic ends.* New York: Norton.

White, M. (2001). Folk psychology and narrative practice. *Dulwich Centre Journal.* 2001. No 2.

White, M. (2007). *Maps of narrative practice.* New York: Norton.

Chapter 10: The effects of Narrative ideas on students' identity and practice

Richard Cook

Introduction

This chapter presents the results of a qualitative study into the effects of learning about Narrative Therapy on the ideas of counselling and faith of Year Three, Bachelor of Counselling students at Bethlehem Tertiary Institute in Tauranga, New Zealand. The institute identifies itself as a Christian, University-level professional education institution. Many of the students in this study came into their third and final year with some suspicions about the post-modern ideas that underpin this modality.

The researchers were staff in the counselling programme: James Arkwright, Michelle Youngs and myself. We were concerned to know what the effects were of this learning on key areas of the students' lives and work. We had ourselves shared some of these suspicions during our own Narrative training and had experienced degrees of resistance and wariness but also of possibility and revelation.

Anecdotal feedback had indicated that as a result of this course in the past, students had an increased awareness of the shaping power of the social context in which they, and clients live. In class they often raised questions about the implications of these ideas for their faith. These interactions piqued our curiosity as to the effects of the Narrative counselling paper on the students over the semester in which it was taught.

The students had already interacted with a range of ideas during their counselling programme. These included the role of language to powerfully prescribe what people perceive reality to be in social context within which they live. This awareness of the shaping power of social messages, norms and expectations (discourses) led on to an examination of the particular discourses that had influenced them in their family of origin and then later to an exploration of the discursive influences in a family in the wider community. A literature review of the ideas underpinning Narrative Therapy had also been completed in order to develop students' awareness of how these identity conclusions and codes for living are shaped and internalised.

Methodology

Against this backdrop, students entered their third and final year of their degree and began the development of Narrative practice in their counselling work. Our purpose for this study was to discover what effects the students in a particular cohort noticed in their thinking about and experience of counselling and faith as a result of their interaction with the ideas underpinning Narrative Therapy.

The methodology was based on Narrative Analysis that explores the experience of people in progress over time in their lived context (Josselson, 2003). This approach studies how people make sense of experience, construct their ongoing sense of self and create meaning for living (Chase, 2003). Akin to Grounded Theory, themes in the Narrative are identified and coded to yield a rich description of the constructions of meaning the participants have produced (Frank, 2005). These are sometimes called schemas for living (Polkinghorne, 1988) and utilise language to create knowledge (Rundblad, 2004). They organise people's "knowledge about and transactions with the social world" (Bruner, 1990, p35). These narratives are seen as "overt manifestations of the mind in action (Chafe, 1990, p79). The stories people tell usually contain the drama of a struggle or tension as people try to integrate new experience into the narrative of their life purpose (Frank, 2005). Sometimes called psycho-discursive practices, these narratives construct "an account of identity...of character...they create realities" (Wetherell & Edley, 1999, p353). Narrative Analysis was seen as a useful strategy for identifying the themes in these students' experience of learning this approach to counselling.

The institute's Ethics Committee approved the study in the knowledge that the researcher directly interacting with the students would not be actually teaching in that course. This was to lessen the possibility that they might express what they thought the teaching staff wanted to hear because they were to be assessing their work since we were asking them to participate in the research at the same time as they undertook the course.

A questionnaire was prepared to be answered three times by those consenting to be involved in the study: before the course began, at its mid-point and at its end. Completed questionnaires were sealed in an envelope and put aside until all the course assessments were marked. This provided one set of data that could potentially indicate students' sense of change over the course.

In order to strengthen the reliability of the analysis, we decided to collect data in two other ways as well. It was hoped that this triangulation would yield themes that were consistent across the group. To that end, a focus group was held at the end of the course and the personal reflections on the impact of the course were completed by the participants as a course assessment. The reflections were retained and studied only when the marks had been returned.

This method gave us our three sets of data to analyse. Each set was then coded by theme and those that were common to all three sets were identified. Being a case study of one particular cohort, the results were considered to be valid because they were personal narratives that were being described by those participants. While this is not necessarily generalisable to other cohorts or to other counsellor education programmes, it does give insight into the effects of these ideas on this group at this time. The study could be replicated with other cohorts or other programmes in the future to see if these effects are more generalisable.

Results

Our research question then was: What are the effects on a group of Christian students' ideas about counselling and faith as they are taught the Narrative approach to therapy?

Effects on students' ideas about counselling

Students consistently spoke of a significant awareness developing as to the dynamics of power in their counselling and personal relationships. They also noticed a growing appreciation of the power of words and their meanings. These awarenesses enabled a lessening of the expert, all-knowing stance as a counsellor. To illustrate, one student said:

I have enjoyed learning how the Narrative approach can rearrange the power dynamics, that the client is the expert on their own life.

Students felt that clients were less dependent on the counsellor and that they were more side by side in a joint venture. It meant that as a counsellor, they did not have to be the sole leader of the process.

There were several statements around an emerging liking of the Narrative modality because they no longer had to "be ahead of the client". This enabled them to be "more relaxed and less assertive", whereas with other modalities they felt they needed to be challenging and confrontational.

I tended to see counselling as formula based. Conversely I would refer to Narrative as an art.

Students commonly expressed feeling more relaxed and freer to be themselves when using a Narrative approach:

It released in me courage and the freedom to be more creative in the sessions.

I've enjoyed learning a therapy which feels more like my personality.

I can decorate my own garden.

I am a fellow traveller.

I am like a Tui {native New Zealand bird} singing in a tree – celebration, freedom, dancing.

In spite of the size of the challenge, students found changes had come that were beneficial to them personally and to their work. They spoke of learning a new language and growing into a new way of thinking.

Narrative has helped me to view a different way of living... a different way of relating and looking at people...

It's like learning a new language... being thrown into a new culture.

They felt that the course had not only given them a new way of seeing clients, but a new way of viewing the world and a new way of thinking about themselves.

Inspired by Narrative ideas, students also reported a growing ability to consider the individual in the larger contexts of their lives. They reported an increased awareness of the power of social discourses:

Having lived under a yoke of oppression I am more knowledgeable of the discourses that shape people.

I am motivated to help my clients recognise where they are oppressed by discourses and attitudes in their life.

It has excited me to witness people gaining a voice.

Attitudes and approaches to the counselling relationship had also changed over the months of the course. The level of curiosity had risen:

Another highlight for me is adopting the stance of curiosity; questioning for more detail in the smaller, average, day to day words.

I believe it is the stance of curiosity that holds the key to unlocking a client's heart…

Students were more aware of their own assumptions and felt that they had been able to decrease their judgement of clients. They found themselves looking for positive threads and subordinated strengths in clients' stories:

…if I discover strength I am curious to know where that strength emerged and what keeps it alive…

Having this "glass half-full attitude" increased students respect for clients:

This is counselling in a way that tries not to be judging, clinical or restricting… that empowers clients.

Another change in stance as a counsellor was centred on how students had come to view the relationship between clients and problems. They reported that speaking of a problem in an externalised way enabled both parties in the counselling relationship to see that the client per se is not the problem:

I like externalising conversations because they see the problem as the problem, not the person as the problem. The conversation can also help examine the cultural, socio-political stories that influence people's lives.

The concept of externalising the problem was very helpful. For the first time in my client's experience, he was able to step aside and begin looking more objectively at its dynamics.

Recently a client at ABC High School commented to me how she liked it that I had not 'bagged' {criticised} her Mum during the session even though she had…. Externalising 'the alcohol' took away judgement.

Students spoke of how going against dominant social judgements supported a commitment to justice. Exploring the relationship between the problem and the client enabled greater patience, honouring and less space for prejudice. To describe this endeavour, students used such metaphors as:

...it's a standing against injustice ...

... mining for gold...

... dusting for clues...

... curiously seeking strengths...

From this stance, student counsellors described themselves as:

A mirror...

An advocate...

A friend...

A curious researcher...

A detective who cares...

A miner looking for gold amidst the dirt...

An archaeologist looking for lost treasure...

These descriptions all point to a changed positioning of the student-counsellor as one alongside, and was preferred by the participants to an "over and above" expert role.

Another change students reported was in what they were paying attention to in the client's story. Some spoke of having deficit thinking so internalised and ingrained that if they had a problem, it meant there was something wrong with them as an individual. Some spoke of formerly seeing counselling as focussing on what was wrong with a person – the deficits. That counselling was about

…taking you to look at the bad – the hopelessness.

Narrative Therapy however, had given students a way of thinking about clients in relationship to a problem dynamic. This view was more conducive to leaving the client in tact, not pathologised and with greater levels of hope.

Narrative kicked in with such a positive impact on the client. She herself began talking of the problem and its 'mates' in an externalised way. What a change in countenance she had.

While some spoke of their sense that they were still very much on the learning pathway and "not there yet", with some still searching around for appropriate questions and a sense of continuity in a Narrative process over time, many spoke of a growing confidence that they were expanding their repertoire of skills:

I'm getting richer, with more tools in the toolbox.

Students spoke of being "fascinated with the ideas" and liked "going against binaries to a gambit of shades". While this challenge was significant, they felt it was worthwhile and enabled one to say it was like

…a symphony slowly coming together, other instruments to be learnt that will add a greater fullness.

Repeatedly, students spoke of being able to see themselves as real counsellors for the first time, of being challenged, stretched, excited and hopeful of things to come.

Effects on students' ideas about their faith

Narrative ideas, based as they are in post-modern philosophy, held a challenge for a significant number of students. Some found there were aspects that were not meshing together by the end of the course. These included a lingering confusion for one as she tried to make sense of the Christian scriptures:

I'm trying to sort out Jesus' respectful stance, which is like Narrative, and yet the Bible has a lot of internalised language which is not like Narrative… It's hard to externalise things regarding character because when God addresses things in character it's about deficits… The Bible doesn't talk about laziness, it talks about lazy people. It sent me to a place of confusion of where it [Narrative] fits in relation to myself.

This student felt a resonance with Narrative ideas in her work but a dissonance with her understanding of Biblical language and emphasis.

As a result of these ideas, other students spoke in various ways of a new-found freedom to reconsider absolutes in their belief systems and to examine them. They appreciated the process because it enabled them to look at where they had received those absolutes from, what life-training had contributed to them and what power dynamics were associated with them. But at the same time, they affirmed that the analysis did not have to undermine their worldview, rather it had the potential to inform it further. They could be free to hold on to viewpoints, but to know why they held them and the effects of speaking about those views in certain kinds of ways.

There is nothing wrong with principles. It is helpful to understand how I arrived at them and why I choose to hold onto them.

One student described this re-examination process using this metaphor:

Black and white absolutes have become softened and somewhat obscured amidst a sea of shades of grey.

Another said that this process had diminished her judgement of others' views and that it
...built up my faith — being non-judgemental was how Jesus related to people.

This parallel between Jesus' stance towards people and the way Narrative fosters relating in an open and accepting way, struck other students as well.

...the respectful, non-pathologising stance of the therapist towards the client I imagine Jesus to be very comfortable with.

I love the strength-focused perspective of this approach and I believe it mirrors the way Jesus views his children.

I can picture Jesus using it [Narrative type practices] as He also views people as separate from the problem. His whole attitude to people is one of being non-judgemental, valuing people and respecting them.

Some students spoke of experiencing a greater sense of agency associated with their own spirituality. This included the ability to deal with personal issues better using externalisation. One felt it helped externalise issues in their own life that enabled them "not to buy back into problem".

Some saw agency as the ability to have ascendancy over the personal and systemic dynamics of evil described as principalities and powers:

I saw how Christianity and Narrative dovetailed and I particularly liked the way agency was given to a person that gave them choice and power to get distance from problems and arguments inspired by principalities and powers.

As the tactics became clear I could feel the fight come back into me and I was ready to go to war on the problem.

Others had personified views of evil and likened the externalising of a problem to the action of "the Devil" or "Satan".

As soon as I saw the issue in a Narrative way, it took the power away. I saw it like the devil… and said "no". Like in class, I saw the devil sucking the life out of me, said "no" and I could stand against it.

…this brings to my attention that there is a spiritual war between God and demons…

I saw the problem like Satan trying to stop me from blooming – thinking of it like this made me adamant to fight with everything I had.

Others spoke of increased agency being very similar to biblical ideas of freedom:

I have learned that Narrative can liberate people.

I feel I have more free will in the sense that I can be aware of such stories and decide which ones work for me.

… not to be enslaved again by the yoke of slavery.

It is wonderful to see a client move from seeing the problem as something within so it can be observed from a safer place…to see how a problem may have robbed someone of freedom to live life more fully.

Agency was further experienced as a sense of growing and expanding, and of challenging binaries:

… I became aware that significant parts of my faith were trapped in a binary of either/or. .. The potential of looking beyond the binary was revealed.

One student put their growing sense of agency in their faith into a poignant metaphor:

A yacht that's been still in the dead calm has now got whispers of wind blowing in the sails and its now moving the yacht slowly forwards - building confidence.

The final aspect to this theme of the effect of Narrative ideas on students' faith is their sense of growth in an interdependent relationship with God. They spoke of feeling shaky about their Narrative practice and how stress sometimes blocks out their sense of God, but of a restfulness that was emerging, a satisfaction that God was present and aiding them, bringing growth, acceptance and affirmation to them. They spoke of feeling inspired and stronger than before and confident about trusting God's love to overcome any timidity that remains.

The colourful metaphors employed to describe themselves in this increasingly agentic relationship with God were like being:

A foetus.

In a flowing river.

A seed opening into a bud.

A flickering tea light.

Conclusion

As researchers who are also Christians and committed to the professional formation of counsellors as disciples of Jesus who can stand in the stream of their own profession as agents of the redemptive work of God in people's lives, these accounts were both gratifying and inspiring. Students were describing many aspects of the life of God seen in the scriptures at work in their lives. They reported a richer experience of life (John 10:10), of God and of faith.

The narrative reflected a number of qualities enhanced by participation in the Narrative counselling course that relate closely to the transforming work of God seen in the Scriptures. Much like the Greek reference to the Holy Spirit (the *paraclete*), they spoke of a sense of coming alongside clients in their lives. They spoke of being less rigid and more accepting (Ref). They reported being more alert to the machinations of power and the ways it can be used to lord it over people (ref) and of an alternative stance of serving others for their good and growth (ref). They experienced a strengthened connection with and dependence on God (ref). They had increased discernment of the conforming powers of the social world (Rom 12:2) and experienced themselves as facilitating clients' agency to grow in freedom from this conformity to be transformed by new ways of thinking and new knowledges of themselves and God's ideas for life. They experienced themselves as less judgemental (Matthew 7:1).

Furthermore, they saw Narrative Therapy as focussing on things that are good, right, pure and lovely (Phil. 4:6) and facilitating the kind of freedom planned for God's people (Gal 6). They found this way of being more respectful than they had known (1 Peter 2:17). They were clearer about principles to live by rather than laws to obey (Romans 8). They found themselves valuing the wonderful creation that human beings are (Ps 139), a strengthened spiritual resistance (Eph 6) and a way of enabling freedom from slavery (Rom 6-7).

This study confirmed for us that learning Narrative Therapy had the potential to advance the work of God as described in the scriptures in students' and clients' lives. Furthermore, it encouraged us that Narrative Therapy is a useful tool for the Christian and wider community to experience the transformative power of God.

References

Bruner, J. (1990). *Acts of meaning*. Cambridge, MA: Harvard University Press

Chafe, W. (1990). Some things that narratives tell us about the mind. In B. Britton & A. Pellegrini, *Narrative thought and narrative language*. Hillsdale, NJ.: Lawrence Erlbaum

Chase, S. (2003). Learning to listen. In R. Josselson, A. Lieblich, & D. McAdams, (2003). *Up close and personal*. Washington: APA Press

Frank, A. (2005). *Narrative inquiry: Selves, experience and story*. Paper presented at the Research symposium, AUT, Auckland, New Zealand. 13-14th July, 2005.

Josselson, R. (2003). Introduction. In R. Josselson, A. Lieblich, & D. McAdams, (2003). *Up close and personal*. Washington: APA Press

Polkinghorne, D. (1988). *Narrative knowing and the human sciences*. Albany, N.Y.: State University of New York Press.

Rundblad, G. (2004). *Authority in conceptual space: A cognitive discourse analysis approach*. Paper presented at the International Conference on Language, Culture and Mind, Portsmouth 2004.

Wetherell, M., & Edley, N. (1999). Negotiating hegemonic masculinity: Imaginary positions and psycho-discursive practices. *Feminism & Psychology, 9*(3), 335-356.

Chapter 11: Christians using Narrative Therapy with children

Richard Cook with Su Fenwick and Michelle Youngs

About the practitioners

Su Fenwick works in a private practice collective with children, adolescents and adults. She also works in a church context offering groups for women living in violent situations or coming out of living in violence, and also at a primary school with children facing complex issues. Su has worked in counselling and teaching within primary and secondary schools. Su has two adult children and a history of working with abuse and trauma.

Michelle Youngs works in the same private practice collective with equal time spent counselling children, adolescents and adults. She also works with families in a Christian school. She is married, has two young boys and has worked in high school teaching and counselling, in tertiary lecturing and supervision.

Introduction

Narrative Therapy has a long history of work with children and with children in the context of their families and lends itself to this work because it can be an experimental and creative process. Narrative has also been combined with art and drama by various practitioners bringing play, role play, art, sand play, the use of props and expressive processes into the relationship. In this way, the meaning-making embedded in the stories children tell, can be represented when words themselves are not available or sufficient.

This chapter documents an interview with two practitioners working with children and young people. They discuss their work using Narrative ideas and describe their understanding of Jesus' heart and relational style towards children. They articulate what it means to connect, engage and work intentionally with a child while being acutely aware of their contextual landscape and the way in which power positions both the child and the counsellor. Three ideas are in focus which inform their work and facilitate change: that the child has a new experience of themselves within the counselling relationship; that 'bearing witness' to children's experience, and the meaning they make of it, is paramount; and that where the child's context is unable to be changed, their relationship to it can be. These ideas are illustrated through examples from their work. In all cases, names have been changed to ensure confidentiality.

The two practitioners interviewed here have extensive experience of a range of creative approaches in their work with children.

Giving options

Richard: What are some of the key aspects for you in working with children and young people?

Michelle: The first time you meet a child normally the first focus is the other adults in the room. We are intentional in our first focus being the child who is greeted and spoken to first.

The other practice that's quite important is very early on opening up a freedom and permission for choice and permission, working in ways that get a child to verbalise or do things that are outside of the good, right, correct box.

Su: Very often in the first few sessions, in our games and conversations, I invite the children to begin to talk about things where there are going to be small disclosures. So I'll ask things like, "Who is your best teacher, and who is your worst?" Even in asking who's the worst there's an answer to give. I haven't verbalized, 'Look, you can tell me anything'. Instead it's in my approach and questions that I give them permission to speak. I may make them the boss of the whiteboard because normally what child controls the whiteboard pen? They get to choose the tangible things they want to use – for example the magnets or the puppets. They're beginning to get an experience of choice.

Michelle: Then it's about acknowledging why they're there. That's important otherwise often the child is confused and doesn't know how to act. I will say that to them, "Look I know Mum and Dad are worried about the anger that you're dealing with, but I wonder if we just put the anger over to one side, over in a cupboard just for a minute because I'd like to get to know about you, what your favourite stuff is." It's taking the time to work away from the problem because then there's actually more scope for change because we're starting to show that we know their identity is not 'the problem'. It's clarifying an identity that's strong enough to fight this particular problem. This is the alternative view emerging. How they are away from the problem? Is this the better side of who they are, who in fact they're created to be?

I find that about 30 or 40 minutes is usually enough for a session. I often use the whiteboard to plan slots of time particularly for children who function well with structure. One slot might be my topic, one might be their turn. It might be to share something good that happened this week or it might be talking about social skills we're working on. It might be to play a certain game. Then we change turns by the clock because they understand that. But you have to be intentional and you have to be clear, "It's my turn now and I want to talk about…"

Connection

Su: Working with children is very different to working with adults because you can't rely on language as your prime way of communicating. The child's language is still developing. It's more important that a cord of connection is there with a child.

I see counselling with all people, but children in particular, as a rope with three cords. One cord is the knowledge we have from learning. The second is the cord of experience – both life and professional experience. These two chords get inter-twined in the work. But I believe there's a third chord which comes from the heart. It's the heart and spiritual connection - love, empathy and respect. It's the twining of that rope that forms the connection with another person. I see it as a hollow rope and in the middle of the rope there's a flowing, an actual vibrancy of connection. It's in that place that I believe the work is done. The rope is not a formula; it's actually a living thing.

A child lives in the now. When a child is in the now with you, they're connected. If there's something they want to say, they will come out and say it without being aware of the consequences of what they're saying, whereas an adult will often tell you something, but they will have thought about it and about the impact of what they might be saying. A child might say something completely unaware of the impact of what they're disclosing and you've got to hold that and work with that in a connection that doesn't make them more unsafe or more exposed.

Michelle: I think this is where Jesus' ideas and Narrative ideas really interface. Children can experience themselves differently when they're heard and validated this way. I had one young girl who was extremely traumatised. Fifteen minutes into the session she just said, "It's so warm in here". I've had that experience before where children try to verbalise this feeling of nurture. It's not anything to do with the physical heat. It's a knowing of nurturing love. I think that when a child knows that this person really likes them and is genuinely interested in knowing how they are and what's going on, it changes them. Some of the good things that make us who we are and the fact that someone else likes me can nurture an alternative identity story that, "Maybe I'm likeable".

To be interested in what a boy did about a problem issue and how he made a "good choice" may seem just a small moment of time, but the message is - their small choices matter to me. The chance to tell about it thickens the story.

We are a witness to the worth of this child and it's incredibly valuable. That seems to be where the alternative story of another side of themselves starts to emerge. Often that part hasn't been given permission to be exposed and I think there's potential there for that part to start to emerge and to be translated into other contexts.

Su: Jesus prioritized the people without a voice, the people who were downtrodden, who were marginalized. A child's voice is often the one that is unheard, and Jesus' emphasis epitomizes to me the priority we should place on children. Matthew 18:10 has transformed my view of working with children. It says, 'See that you do not look down on one of these little ones, for I tell you that their angels in heaven see the face of my Father." I want to treat every child with that dignity and respect because children have that access to the Father, some vision or privilege that I don't have. I don't see children treated as a gift by many people in their lives and I think I need to treat them as a gift. This helps me to see children a little more through God's eyes.

This changes the whole positioning. On earth here, the adults are top and children are lesser, that's the way the differential is. But in the kingdom of heaven, it's the other way around. So, it's about seeing their value, hearing what they want to say and staying where the child is at.

I sometimes just have to look at the child and think, "What is your angel doing now? That just turns it around straight away for me. The problem stops being central then. I think there's a connection that happens at a spiritual level. When I see a child who is being abused physically or sexually I wonder about their angel in tatters and my heart just goes out. What's the impact on those angels around a child who is being so hurt? What's the impact on their cry to God?

With this kind of positioning and connection there can be some exposure. A boy I worked with began to tell me that he saw his uncle being shot. Because we were connecting, it just came out. But it happened when he was three. He didn't know it, but that trauma of seeing the gun put to his uncle's head shocked him into the angry way he was in the world.

We might know by watching that something has happened, but you can't know what particular experience has happened. You have to wait until that child tells you. You're exploring the context all the time, with that real interest in their life and in what's going on. The minute it happens, it's almost like the air in the room changes. It might be a comment like, "My dog died," but you know, because of everything that happens in that room that this is incredibly important, but you've got to be in that place first to recognise it.

Michelle: It's because relevance is very important, being interested in what they're interested in and having props and resources to start to link to that. Finding out if the guys are into motorbikes and military aircraft might lead to making paper planes. It's finding what they connect with, what their world is made up of and trying to enter into that as much as you can. It also makes it fun.

Humour too is a huge part of the work, because quite frankly the kids won't want to come back if they feel like they're being interrogated. But if they come knowing they're going to be with someone who likes them and that they're going to do things that they're interested in doing, they'll want to come. And in that wanting to come back they'll hopefully be willing divulge more of what's going on inside.

And I think God is interested in who we are, in re-creating our identity through transformation so he's interested in who this child is becoming, or who this child could be without this difficulty.

I think that the child is active in there too, trying to tell us things sometimes but not knowing how. Sometimes they just enjoy being there. One girl I worked with would dance around because she had such a freedom to do that. She did cartwheels in the room! She could just be free to be enjoyed and laughed with. For her, this was a completely different experience of herself. That speaks to me of freedom - the freedom of God, and the freedom of total acceptance.

What is the child doing? Something different from what they normally do, having a different experience of themselves because of the freedom and unconditional acceptance. And I need to widen the context to identify others who can or do give that kind of feedback too.

The influence of context

Michelle: The power of the context in which they live makes work with children very different. You can't divorce the child from their family and the wider context. Often the child will come with very strong voices from parents and other adults that have defined them as problematic. They come with stories about themselves that are pathologising and there are agendas of how you should help this child.

Su: Often people are caring and concerned with a strong interest in progress and a huge ability to input into that child's life. In working with the child you've got to be able to work with the adults in their life if long term change is going to happen.

Working with the context that the child lives in is a significant challenge. You can't often change that context, but you can change their relationship to it, and give them a different experience of themselves.

Children are influenced so much by their environment and they seem to carry and express a lot of the emotional climate of the family. So in a sense often the children are the emotional barometer. We help to sift out where the emotions belong. So often a child is saying something but it's being said behaviourally and it's interpreted by an adult as the child's problem and we need to unpack that with the parent too.

Interacting with parents makes confidentiality difficult. I think it is very important to establish parameters for confidentiality when the counselling is first set up. I meet with parents first so they have an opportunity to express what their concerns are for the child, without the child hearing all of that. This allows us to validate that parent's experience and to begin to start to work with it. We can present questions that help them to start to think differently about this child, about the child's strengths and preferences. If we give adequate time to the parent, then they're less likely to feel they have to be over-involved in the therapy. We talk about confidentiality and reassure them that they are very much part of the process.

We have review times when we meet with them to update them about how things are going and there are times when we will include them in work with the child. I'll say things like, "I'll talk to the child about ways we can feed back to you so you know what's going on". There are some exceptions to that if there are safety issues that the child's parent has to be aware of. But there are also times when I've fed back to the parent too soon. The changes or ideas are too premature. It's a bit like the parable where the seed is sown on shallow ground and it doesn't have a chance take hold.

Michelle: Parents are often anxious about what might happen to their child or what the child might say or disclose. This vulnerability needs reassurance at the outset. Where possible we will resource the child to tell the parents what they need to, rather than us being the conveyor.

The Narrative ideas in this work

Richard: What are some important Narrative ideas for you in working with children?

Michelle: I love the story metaphor - that people's lives are made up of stories. Often people say "that's just the story of my life." These stories can define somebody, so I love the idea of helping people to re-story themselves differently. Re-story themselves not just how they would prefer to be, but I think how God intended them to be.

Narrative ideas are a way of seeing the social world. It's a way of seeing people, life and experiences. It's a way of seeing pain. It's a way of seeing shame. It's a way of seeing the negative and the scary and the dark in emotions and experiences. I don't see a person as pain. I see the pain and the shame being things that they contend with or burdens that they carry. These things are not who people are or who they were created to be. They're things that have come in as a result of their experiences or trauma.

I also see Narrative ideas as a way of fleshing out some of the God-ideas that I hold. I see counselling as trying to help people be restored into God's image, to experience life and relationship with God as it was designed to be. So that's about me having a walking and talking relationship with Jesus and helping clients to not continue under the influence of sinful ideas – the negative discourses of the culture. It's helping to restore the innocent, pure part of the child.

Richard: Does that relate to restoring the agency of a child?

Su: Yes it does, and often it means confronting those things that are trying to undermine that agency. Children who for example have been exposed to pornography or experienced abuse or witnessed domestic violence need us to open an alternative landscape to the dominant one they live in, while validating who they are within their current context. Their dominant context, while perhaps being normalised, is not necessarily the preferred one. The child may need support to realise this and to develop a different relationship to this difficult context.

One of the questions I remember I was really struggling with when I was studying was the idea of externalising the problematic and significant experiences or feelings: how do I externalise the weight of sadness I feel. I don't want to externalise it because I feel it. My tutor asked me, "Where do you feel that weight?" I said, "Right here in my gut and it feels too minimising to externalize it." She said, "No, you have already externalised it because you've talked about the sadness. You are not the sadness. You are Su, and you carry that." I began to see that pain and a lot of other really dark and heavy emotions and the meanings that come out of negative and hurtful and traumatic experiences are what we carry, not who we are.

Richard: How does that fit with ideas you have about following God and Jesus and his ideas?

Su: Because I see that He wants me to get free of the burdensome things I carry. I don't believe He just lifts it right off and you're all fancy free. But it means that who I am is not all that big bad pain. That separates the identity of me from the weight of what I carry. I can see the weight of things and the negative-ness of things that people carry as a result of experiences rather than as a result of being intrinsically at fault or being born like that.

One of the big realisations for me was that God himself has created me and that is who I go back to. My time on earth is only a part of my whole life. So in terms of the trauma, pain and negative experiences in this life, it was the realisation that I don't have to be trapped in those. I don't have to be identified according to those. I could get to know a God who is so incredibly real that he is taking those things off. It's like when Jesus says, "Come to me all you who are weary, and heavy laden. Take my yoke upon you and learn from me for yoke is easy and my burden is light…" The things that weigh us down, the things that we see we are, these can be removed. We are not those things. Narrative ideas help me identify the burdens separately from the person and help to change the relationship with the difficulty.

One of my clients came in and she had broadcasted on the internet, "I am. I am X. I am not BPD." She had a whole lot of diagnoses yet she had that huge awareness of being able to separate herself from her diagnoses and come into that place of knowing who she was.

Richard: So, that idea that a person is not the burden or label they're carrying, is that a Narrative idea or is that a Biblical idea?

Su: Both. One of the underpinning beliefs in Narrative is that you are not those totalising ideas of saying for example, "I am shy". Narrative will look at that shy-ness as being separate from who you are. In all that God says and all that Jesus teaches is the love that he has for us and ways in which to separate and set aside the things we carry that weigh us down. In Narrative, when we look at the person we help them externalise those things that weigh them down.

Richard: So these are not just Narrative ideas but somehow they're Narrative ideas and Christian ideas about working with children coming together?

Michelle: They inform each other somehow. Ultimately it's that Jesus is the only one who can restore, and to me that's my under girding idea. So that creates hope. Narrative helps me to articulate this hopefulness and optimism and put it into action. There's an idea in Narrative that there will be moments of exception. There will be threads of something different and that's where I see Jesus at work. God's touch on that person's life might have gone unnoticed, but I see Narrative as highlighting 'God's fingerprints' on someone's life.

Su: I think they're God moments, or rather threads - alternative stories that are made up of many moments. And these storylines will be different from the way that a person or a child has seen themselves. I think they show a glimpse of God at work.

Change

Richard: What's your experience of how change comes about when you work with children?

Michelle: For me change is about change at the identity level – their sense of themselves - rather than the behavioural level. So often the child may report that they've stopped swearing at their mother or hitting the teacher, but it's more about how they view themselves. We use games and activities that help to gain insight into how that view of themselves might have changed – like using puppets and dolls to identify how they feel now. Scaling tools are useful too to see how life has changed for them. A consistent view of themselves that's different would indicate to me a long term change rather than just a behavioural change.

Richard: How do you see God at work in those moments?

Su: Let me give you an example. If I think of a child who's managed to do something different or see something different in the hard time, if they have found courage or found ways to speak up when they're being put down, they are empowered moments. God designs us to be people of courage and hope and resilience and it's in those moments when God brings revelation to that child. So I believe that in those moments it's the Holy Spirit creating change because only he can create change in the way we see things and in the way we are.

It's light versus darkness. There is light in each child. Their view of themselves can be dark because they've been boxed as a problem or they live in a box of darkness because of their context, or both. But it's finding where God's light is in that and helping that child to experience that life differently, with some hope, with some promise, with something to live for.

Michelle: Often I talk with children about having a shield in front of them to block the arrows of hurt that may want to come and destroy them, and what is that shield. If they are a God-follower, I ask how Jesus can be that shield for them.

This is a three way partnership! My role as a counsellor is finding out what is God up to here, and trying to be part of that. That sort of moment when the child tells the crux of what's behind whatever is happening, to me that's a God moment! So it's asking God, "What change are you bringing about in this child's life? How can I be part of facilitating that? How can I create an environment in which that can happen?" It's very much a partnership.

Building an audience

Su: Drawing on Narrative ideas, we want to build an audience to the changes that the child is making. It might be a particular decision or strategy for the child to deal with something or somebody. So in the room we begin to identify an audience to the developments. If not the parent, sometimes I will bring in someone whom that child is happy to tell about a disclosure or a development. It starts with me speaking first and I often say, "Well I'm going to begin talking but if I get it wrong will you help me out." In about two sentences the child picks it up and you've got them starting to tell.

Michelle: It might be more imaginary. "If so and so were here what might you want them to know?" It's giving the child a sense of an audience to view or appreciatively hear what's been developing. You're scaffolding the child towards being able to have more agency in their own lives; building the language to speak what they need to say. This gives them an emotional language and scaffolds them to become surer of themselves in this world.

The counsellor not as expert

Michelle: Instead of the counsellor coming with expert knowledge, and trying to persuade or coerce a client to go down a particular path, a key Narrative idea I value is coming in more collaboratively, respecting the client's knowledge of themselves, but realising too that I have something to offer the process.

Su: I believe it allows a lot more of God to move because I am not in a head space of what needs to happen next, I'm more in a heart place.

Michelle: Narrative ideas help us be especially aware of the power dynamic. I try to reduce the power differential by being transparent myself in a two way process. So, if we play a game, I reveal something of myself too. We might play emotional naughts and crosses, where children have to identify a feeling and say when they felt like that. I'll play that too and I'll equally share examples from my current experience and from when I was a child so that they can identify with my emotions as well. I join in with dressing up and role play. There's still structure and intentionality but I'm going with the process. And there are ideas around how to play safely and not to hurt each other but at the same time there's freedom to experiment.

Su: In terms of the Narrative ideas, I'm interested in exploring the landscape of this child's life and family. I'm interested in knowing how it is to be this ten year old child. Not just any ten year old, not just any ten year old girl, not how it is to be ten year old girls in general, but how it is to be <u>this</u> ten year old girl. This enables me to go slow and to stay with the small details of their experience.

The Narrative perspective gives permission to not be the expert about their life. If she's talking about feeling mad, I can assume how ten year old girls might feel mad and what it might look like in action, but we actually spend a lot of time deconstructing that. In her beginning to find the words it positions me as not knowing how her experience is - the naïve enquirer, the non-expert about her experience of anger.

Michelle: But it's very tentative work because you can't put words in their mouths or build a language that's how you might see it to be. I talked with a child who had "a sore tummy". To be able to find out that this sore tummy was there because of an anxiousness about something completely different to the presenting issue meant not saying, "Have you got a sore tummy because of a, b or c", because they might just say yes to give you the answer they think you want. It's their description and their meanings that are important to draw out.

Su: Although Jesus held so much knowledge there was no sense of condescension or of that 'expertness' being imposed on anyone around him. The most knowledgeable person in the whole world at that time stopped his disciples from sending away children when all the adults wanted to see him. He had a lot to do but he wanted to spend time with a child.

An example from practice

Su: As an example, there's a Pacific Island child I've worked with who is currently living in a very difficult situation where there's a lot of abuse and gang involvement. Through the conversation she said that what she does is pray to Jesus. She doesn't go to Church; they're not a Christian family. I asked her, "What did she think Jesus might think or what he might say back?" She said she couldn't say but could she write it? So she got the whiteboard and she wrote down: "He would say 'I feel sorry for that poor little girl. I would have liked to help her.'" So she had a concept already of a Jesus who was concerned for her, who cared for her. From that base I could wonder with her about why he would say that. Would he care about this person, about her feelings? Now she knew more that this distant person might say.

This helped her build a huge resource because she's living in a family and a place where no one is safe. So then I became a butterfly on the wall of her house. I asked what I might see. Now she had two voices. She had her concept of Jesus and what he might say and she had what this butterfly might say to some of these people. She began to look at alternatives to the situation she's in and began to see what someone else might say about it. I didn't want her to go out and say that to the real people because it would place her in extreme danger. We were looking at a whole different realm.

Richard: In her work with you, your sense is God's desire would be that she has a different story, she knows something different about herself?

Su: Yes, that by experiencing herself differently with me she's been able to talk about the abuse-laden landscape. Once we've talked together about her in that landscape, she's not an isolated person where no one knows what's going on. Now she knows other voices that speak into who she is in that context. She can then have a different experience of herself in the abuse-laden landscape in which she lives.

Richard: Through the butterfly, you and your voice, through the Jesus presence and his voice?

Su: And then finding ways that she can remember those voices and even wondering if there are still other voices. We can look at the concept of a fairy godmother or angels or other voices that might sustain her.

Johnella Bird says that we should accord the same respect to a child's imaginary world, as we do to an adult's recollections of their childhood. We can listen to a child's imaginary world and judge it as not really real. So when we're working with the butterfly which is an imaginary place in their mind, or with a magic carpet they fly on, this imaginary world needs respect.

Richard: So that's coming out of the ideas that there's another story about this girl that God would long for this girl to know.

Su: Yes, an alternative understanding and meaning – an alternative story. It gives her a sense that instead of isolation there's now an audience, a community of support and this can resource children in the difficult contexts in which they live, long after they leave our room.

Conclusion

Richard: Thank you for passing on your insights about working Narratively with children. If I could summarise, I think you're saying that as Christians who have interacted with Narrative ideas Jesus' way of encountering children has inspired you. He brought them close, he privileged them. Children were marginalised in society anyway, along with all the other people that Jesus spent time with, and that this has given you a set of ideas or discourses to inform your practice. The first glance, the first interaction, the connecting with them around their interests and structuring sessions around them is the outworking of this.

Then your ideas as Christians about what God is up to is that he has this longing for transformation and restoration of all people. This inspires in you a longing to reflect to the child the identity that he sees, the truth of how he sees them and the good that he has for their life.

Through that stance in your conversations you are listening for those moments where the burden that they're carrying comes out and they're confident enough to speak about it and how they're making sense of that burden. For you, that's a Narrative externalising of it. But it's also in line with what you understand God's purpose is. You listen for those other moments where his light is - moments of alternative identity experience where they are a little freer of the burden and where there's some alternative action.

So in all those intentional things you're doing your faith is active. You believe that God's heart wants this child to have the opportunity to experience something different, to be somebody different, and to have more agency to do some things differently as a result.

Su: Yes, a lot of it is inspiring hope. We're planting seeds of possibility and trusting the Gardener to help them grow.

Chapter 12: Narrative ideas & practices in pastoral care and counselling

Irene Alexander with John Silver and Jo-anne Brown

About the authors

John Silver

I am a pastor who feels very passionate about helping people to achieve spiritual and emotional wholeness. A passion that came as God challenged me about ministering to the "bruised reeds and smouldering wicks" (Isaiah 42:3) of the world, those men and women who were struggling to make sense of their situation and to experience some level of wholeness in their spiritual relationship with God and in their emotional health. I see it as a call to identify with the words of Jesus in Mark 6:34 where he and his disciples encounter a large crowd who were seeking him. Mark records that Jesus was moved by their plight. He saw them as "sheep without a shepherd", lost, vulnerable and needing someone to journey with them as a guide and support, to help them become strong and healthy. I have been involved in Pastoral ministry as both student and Pastor for about fifteen years in Baptist churches in Brisbane, Australia. I have a Graduate Diploma in Ministry and a Master of Counselling.

Jo-anne Brown

I am a Salvation Army Officer and am committed to ministering healing and wholeness to the people I encounter - in my environment as well as in my Church. Along with my husband, I have been in ministry in both Australia and Germany for over 17 years. Our desire, whether we are in Australia or the former East Germany, is to provide a place where people feel accepted and welcomed, and where they can experience the love of Jesus Christ. I have a Diploma of Primary and Special Education, a Diploma of Missiology, and a Master of Counselling.

Introduction

Pastoral care and counselling includes a plethora of counselling and care ministries that share in common a unique blend of factors - the nature of the pastoral relationship and the issues of spiritual life, especially the implications of faith and hope in the person's everyday life. Being a Christian is about joining my story with the narrative of God who is seeking to redeem people who freely respond to the offer of salvation made through the life, death and resurrection of Jesus Christ. Often people who come for pastoral counselling recognise that they have lost contact with God, that is, they are not in step with God's narrative. Using Narrative Therapy allows us to use techniques like deconstruction, externalising and restorying people's identities in accordance with their understanding of their relationship with Jesus Christ. This chapter explores some of the ways pastors and pastoral counsellors can utilise Narrative Therapy concepts and processes.

Narrative Therapy and pastoral ministry

Both John and Jo-anne were involved in pastoral ministry before they encountered Narrative Therapy in their Masters degrees in Counselling. Studying in different institutions and involved in different denominations they were both challenged by ideas they saw as consistent with their understanding of Jesus, but different from previous perceptions. As they continued to engage with Narrative ideas while maintaining pastoral work – preaching as well as pastoral care – they pondered on ways these ideas could enhance their practice and engagements with those with whom they worked.

Irene: How has Narrative Therapy changed your relationship with those you encounter in the pastoral role?

> John:
> In the traditional role of the pastor, you're expected to solve the problem. In a narrative approach the

emphasis is on a more collaborative, non expert position. I'm able to ask, "Well what do you think? Have you had other experiences similar to this one?" I can draw from them their strengths, things that they know already that will help resolve the situation.

I have redefined my role of pastor from being the "expert" to seeking to be more of a fellow journeyer in seeking to live out my part in Gods narrative. I still have the positional power inherent in the role by virtue of the specialised knowledge I have, but seek to use that as a resource that I can offer to people who seek answers. Instead of being the expert, I seek to enable, to try and empower people to talk about their stories, valuing their stories and listening to what they are saying.

Narrative has given me a lot more opportunity to sit back and say I don't have to have the answers, to solve their problems. It's given me the opportunity to relax in counselling. I recognize that I can only walk with a person, honouring their story, not solve their problems for them, and only point them toward true emotional and Spiritual wholeness in Christ Jesus.

Jo-anne:
My desire in my ministry is to provide a place where people feel accepted and welcomed, and where they can experience the love of Jesus Christ. Christ himself took a decentred, but influential stance in his dealings with all kinds of people, (although he has the right to claim central position), and treated with the greatest respect those who, from society's viewpoint, were least deserving of respect. Christ had a way of seeing the alternate story and bringing it into the light, and thus into being.

Although I am in Christ and he is in me, I am not Christ and can only ever know part of the truth (as through a glass darkly, 1 Corinthians 13:12). This guards my attitude from becoming judgmental or condemning of those whose concept of truth may differ from mine. It also reminds me that underlying every story, every version of truth, every form of knowing, is God's Truth and God's unchanging story of redemption, hope and renewal. God grant me the eyes to always see it.

Because Jo-anne and John were already pastors when they were learning about Narrative Therapy they were applying Narrative ideas to pastoral ministry. They both also trained as counsellors and wrestled with these dual roles. Students are confronted with the ideas of dual relationships that is relating to people in two different contexts. Usual ethical practice is to avoid dual relationships or to at least be aware of the complications that two parallel relationships cause. Relating to someone as a counsellee and then preaching to them on Sunday as one of the congregation has its own hazards. Additionally pastoral care is more likely to be the day to day interest in the wellbeing of parishioners whereas counselling is engaging with deeper and more long-term issues. I asked Jo-anne and John how they had seen these two roles they now found themselves in.

Irene: How do you handle the dual roles of pastor and counsellor?

Jo-anne: Now I am completing my Master in Counselling degree I can comment specifically on some of the overlap I have found in the counselling and pastoral roles.

As pastor, I am committed to helping people deepen their relationship with God, and so be able to see God at work in their lives. "Uncovering the story of God's work in a client's life" (King, 1999, p. 35) is also what a counsellor does. To be always aware that God is doing something, (even, or perhaps especially, in the midst of difficulties) and to be committed to discovering what that is, is for me the overlap between the two ways of being.

I was drawn by these thoughts to pictures I have seen of Monet's paintings of his water lily garden. The dominant colours on the canvas are darker, deeper colours, which alone would be overwhelmingly gloomy. These colours, however, form the background for the glorious colours of the water lilies, which draw the eye and lift the spirit. Such a concept allows a person to focus on the God-colours in a story or situation, rather than on the problem-colours.

The end result in Monet's painting is something quite exquisite and breathtaking. The end result of this narrative approach in a person's life is hope – which can also be quite breath-taking.

The role of the counsellor as "collaborator with the client" (p. 35), rather than the expert reminded me of the place of the Holy Spirit in a believer's life – also something of a collaborator, working to guide the believer into all truth (John 16:13). The Holy Spirit never forces or pushes (although He is the holder of truth), but takes a decentred, influential position in a person's life – until He is invited into central position. Even then, He works with grace – isn't this what respect is all about? As King used the analogy of "shining a torch" (p. 35), the position of the Holy Spirit was again highlighted for me. "Shining a torch" seems very analogous with "guiding into all truth".

As pastor and counsellor, in my ways of being with people on their spiritual journey, I see the possibility of the Holy Spirit working through me to shine His torch into the stories of people's life. The key is for me to be aware of what He is doing, to know that God is already at work, and to be committed to being the outer casing of the torch through which His light shines. This blurs the line a little between pastor and counsellor, because this is not something I only want to do when I am counselling a client, or when pastoring a member of my church, but a way of being where God always has the freedom and the opportunity to use me to show His light and love to others.

There are clearly times when a counsellor, as simply 'counsellor,' is needed. There are also clearly times when a pastor, to pray and give spiritual guidance, is needed. But more and more, people who approach me for 'counselling' are actually seeking to see more of God at work in their lives and to find God-ways to deal with difficult situations – and God's way to live.

Having said this, I in no way wish to imply that I think I will be the answer to every person and every situation! I am simply acknowledging that having to choose either the role of pastor *or* the role of counsellor (either/or) seems rather modernist in outlook and I believe I would prefer to work in the blurrier world of both/and, and with the help and guidance of the Holy Spirit, hold loosely the tension this brings.

John

Although I had been a pastor for over twelve years I decided to train as a counsellor, completing my Master of Counselling degree, as a response to the challenge I found in the words of Wayne Oates (1959). He said that pastors don't have a choice between counselling or not counselling, but either counselling in a disciplined and skilled manner or counselling in an undisciplined and unskilled manner. I chose the former path with the intention of developing a personal counselling framework that integrated both my ministry and counselling passions.

As I have thought about the dual role of counselling and being a pastor I have come to see that it is not just a dual role, it is often a 'quadruple' one!

Irene:
How has Narrative therapy specifically influenced your understanding of the dual – quadruple role of being a pastor/counsellor?

John:
Especially respect for the person's story, seeing each person as unique – allowing their story to be able to unfold. To give people space – that they don't have to conform in a certain way just because it's a pastor they're talking to. So it's stepping back from that positional power and allowing some agency to develop around people's own stories and perceptions. That's the framework that I have sought to develop. When people see me in other settings they don't see me as the fixer, it breaks down the stereotypes.

Irene
It sounds as though Narrative Therapy has influenced your understanding of the person, and the person's journey. Could you say some more about that?

Jo-anne:
Vitz's discussion of "development of stories about the patient's future" (1996, p.17) highlighted for me the power we all have to shape our future. This seems particularly true for those who consciously allow God to be part of that shaping and direction. The idea of developing future stories (in Vitz's article confined within the context of therapy, but for me in the broader context of pastoral ministry that includes counselling) resonates strongly with me because of where I am in my life at the moment.

I am very conscious of being poised on a knife-edge. On one side is the past story, with its experiences of failure and fear, and the other side beckons with its story of promise and hope. Even this is illusion. The past story does indeed hold threads of promise and hope – as the future story is tinged with failure and fear. In a sense I can choose what this next chapter is to be. The events are obviously not all within my realm of choosing, but the possibility of seeing the promise and hope within those events is.

John:

One of the big things about Narrative where some lights came on, where Narrative Therapy and theology came together for me, was that the story about Christianity is God's narrative. Along the way people have been drawn into that narrative. One of the things I have been captured by is Paul's concept of being in Christ. We join ourselves with Christ in relationship; we become part of the body of Christ in a mystical spiritual connection. The reality in Jesus' words – you give up your life to gain life. Making that commitment to relationship with Christ - which Paul describes as being in Christ – beginning to live the life of the future now.

For me being a Christian is how I take my part in God's bigger narrative. And I choose to join my local narrative with God's narrative. It's helped me to understand sin and dysfunction – they are ways people have dropped out of step with God's narrative.

I see people as spiritual and mental and physical. Every person has a need to fulfil that spiritual response. And the pastor is helping people to connect or reconnect with God's narrative. Christianity is not just accepting propositional truths, but entering into a reciprocal relationship with the person that those propositions are about. At its core Christianity is very narrative. It's less about adhering to propositional truths. Rather those truths have to be lived out in relationship with God.

I've been challenged that in our western secular mindset we have separated knowing and living out what we know. In the Hebrew world, from my understanding, you can't disconnect those – to know something is to live it out. If it's a part of me it will show in how I live. Narrative has challenged me about getting people to look at the bigger picture. When you see your story as a narrative, you can ask 'what's caused me to step out of the narrative, to step away from what I once knew'.

Irene:
How is that idea different from the idea that "God has a plan for your life"?

John:
I'm really uncomfortable with a restrictive view that God has one plan where and we have to search for it to find peace and happiness. I want to step back from that. Maybe to say it like this – God started with a picture of what it would be like to have a group of people in relationship with each other and with God. God started that narrative with two people, then expanded it to a family, a nation, then extended the invitation through Jesus, the exact image of the Father so people could get a sense of the Father. Jesus invites us into a relationship, and in that relationship God challenges us as to how we're going to live and use the abilities and opportunities God gives us. The way I see it is that God has a general will that everyone will come into relationship. "Love God with all your heart and love your neighbour as yourself." A narrower sense of God's will is that God has specific roles for people at times.

Sometimes people have chosen to step away from God's narrative, but sometimes it's something that's happened to them – like abuse. There was one young girl, she was raped, and got involved with a paedophile, really struggled to see herself as someone who was worthwhile. So sometimes people are robbed of a sense of self by the things that have been done to them. It's not just that they 'choose to sin' as theology or the church might seem imply.

Sometimes as a pastor I'm helping people reconnect with the narrative and sometimes I'm helping people who have never seen themselves as a part of God's story. Then the question is, "What would God's story bring to their life?" As a Christian pastoral counsellor it's easier to bring that side into it. People come seeking something, some intuitive voice that perhaps a pastor can help. A pastor has a position where they are part of that whole framework. I might ask "Do you have a sense of where God is?" or, "How does God see that situation?" or, "Where do you think God was when that was happening?" Sometimes abuse has been overlaid with religious things, like where the person who was abusing was religious or in a religious role. That creates all sorts of confusion - as if God is seen to be approving their painful experience. God is the last person they want to invite into their experience. That's why I see abuse from that power position as reprehensible because it not only attacks the person's feelings about themselves but also their sense of spiritual identity.

John and Jo-anne had both used Narrative ideas to conceptualise what they did in their pastoral care and counselling relationships they also mentioned that they used some narrative practices.

Irene:
Could you tell me about examples of the use of Narrative practices, in your pastoring role.

John:

Externalising is intrinsic to the scriptures - right from the beginning, Genesis 4, where God says, "Sin is crouching at the door, its desire is for you." All the way through in the New Testament, externalising is not foreign, it's actually quite biblical. "Don't let sin have mastery over you." This other choice is often externalised as an identity waiting to take over. In Narrative terms an identity that wants to create a different identity other than the identity God makes possible.

I was working with a woman who had suffered long term with anxiety. We talked about the story and deconstructed some of the oppressive things that were affecting who she was. One of the ways to do that was to help her to connect with a time when she wasn't anxious. I asked her, "What would it be like to connect with living how you were then? What were you doing then? What role was God playing in your life then? What changed? How can we reconnect with where God was then?"

We only had a few sessions. She had a lot of beliefs around the idea that she wasn't any good. There had been some childhood stuff that had happened that was still very traumatic. More recently she had had some spiritual experiences that had reconnected with some of the voices of her childhood that had said she wasn't very good.

We deconstructed that by my asking "Do you remember what your intentions were?" Just because she'd done something small but was actually quite innocent, her father had called her a rotten, dirty, little mongrel. I asked her how that could be accurate when she was only six. And I asked "Well what does God say about that? How do you think God sees you?" I was bringing God's view up against the other voice. Then we just talked about how Anxiety is always ready to grab hold of her. From that time she has improved a fair bit. She has a lot less problems with Anxiety and is gaining a lot more confidence. There are fewer opportunities for Anxiety to tell lies about her.

A lot of what we did was focusing on her sense of her identity in Christ, how does God see her, how can she begin to use the gifts God has given her without having to listen to the voices that say "You are no good."

I see the process as three parts:
* Deconstructing the problematic and oppressive story/ies in people's emotional and spiritual experience.
 * Enquiring as to God's storying of the person, their self-hood and life, known in both their own experience and the experience of the faith community – a search for exceptions, or 'unique outcomes'.
* The reconstruction of identity and thickening the alternative story, the construction of an appropriate new identity that reflects their new understanding of their identity In Christ.

Irene:
It is obvious that you have applied Narrative ideas to counselling but also to other aspects of church life. How do these ideas relate to the pastoral activities of preaching and teaching?

John:
I see preaching relating to Narrative in several ways. It is deconstructive of unhelpful thinking, of bad scripture interpretation. Then it seeks to give hope of the possibility of stepping into a deeper connection with Jesus Christ. Finally it rebuilds by thickening the story of this new life narrative.

The Deconstructive aspect is the whole sense of changing, getting rid of the things that drag you down, putting off the old, putting on the new in Christ. This is frequently found in the Proverbs and Psalms - the ideas of putting aside one way of being and choosing another, like, "A gentle answer turns away wrath, but a harsh word stirs up anger" (Proverbs 15:1).

One of the other major things is Restorying – creating a new picture. Thickening the story is when a story is told and retold – often from different perspectives or from different people adding their perceptions. In Christian circles it's about being part of the body of Christ, the people who share your life and your story. So the spiritual gifts are to build up the body, to help people thicken the story and grow up into Christ. A major role I see in preaching is deconstructing and beginning the process of rebuilding and thickening this new life narrative. Preaching aims to present different possibilities, to move people to say "Yes I can do that." Preaching is deconstructing, presenting a different story, giving people some resources and some hope that things can be different.

Jo-anne:
It is through the medium of the story, with its possibilities of identification, revelation and personalisation that a person can be lifted away from the problem. I particularly liked the way Nathan told his story (2 Samuel 11:26-27, 12:1-15) in such a way to minimise the arousal of David's defences. This is rather like shining a torch instead of pointing the finger – and as humans, we clearly respond more favourably to light rather than accusation.

This led me to ponder further on the implications of narrative in preaching. This was Jesus' primary way of teaching (e.g., the parables he told) and would have been etched in the minds of those who heard. Kilpatrick's eight factors about the power of narrative (in Vitz, pp 18-20) are equally relevant for the pulpit. I know from my own experience that I am much more likely to become engrossed in an interesting story than in a string of points, regardless of how eloquently they may be strung together. I intend to further explore this in my preaching ministry.

Just as story crosses the boundaries of the events of a person's life, encompassing them within a meaningful whole, so too do the implications of narrative, and the concept of developing the future story, encompass the varying linked and unlinked circles of my life.

Irene
As I have talked with you it has become obvious that Narrative ideas have been very influential in your present perspectives not only in counselling and pastoral care but also in other pastoral activities and in what church life is about. Can you say something more about that?

John:
When I heard about Narrative Therapy, some lights went on around this, and around the importance of community. For too long as Western Christians we have been influenced by an individualistic mindset and not valued the role of the faith community in people's lives. Paul doesn't envisage the possibility of being a Christian outside of a faith community.

Because of the relationships within the community the process that starts in counselling can be supported by the community. There's a role for between sessions - for there to be supportive listening environment and people they can talk to on their journey to wholeness. That could be part of small groups, intentional groups or a normal Bible study groups.

Jo-anne:
For a long time I had been really struggling to fit narrative thinking into the rest of my life. I really liked the ideas behind it and the experience of it in counselling, but I felt that there was a deeper story with it. This way of thinking, perceiving and interacting seemed to hold such exciting opportunities that it must surely fit in other areas of life. I was especially challenged about this because of the

overlapping roles of pastor and counsellor, and because of what I saw in God's Word.

Since I was finding it hard to apply it in the broader context of pastoral ministry, I decided to start at the beginning – God's Word. If narrative ways of relating to people is valid, then the Biblical precedent would show me that – and show me how... And so my mind drifted through Bible stories. One by one they leapt out of my memory. God is a God of narrative. He is a God of the alternate story. He is the God who not only sees the preferred story but brings it into being. He breathes his life and his Spirit into the story.

God looked Sarai...
  And saw not an old, barren woman...
      But Sarah, a princess, and the mother of a nation
      (Genesis 17)
God looked at Gideon...
  And saw not the weakest clan and the least in the family...
      But a mighty warrior, who would save Israel.
(Judges 6)
God looked at David...
  And saw not the youngest, tending the sheep...
      But a man after his own heart. (1 Samuel 13-16)
Jesus looked at Matthew...
  And saw not a tax collector...
      But an apostle, who would be given authority over
demons
        and sickness (Matthew 9,10).
Jesus looked at the woman anointing him...
  And saw not a sinful woman...
      But a woman who loved much
        because she had been given much (Luke 7).

The stories are many and the truth behind them is powerful. Jesus saw things differently. He saw unique outcomes (sometimes before they even occurred) where others pointed the finger. He showed respect, where others showed scorn. He accepted, while others accused.

I realised how these narrative concepts fit in every area of my life. When I refrain from labelling, step back from making judgments, and avoid accusation – in short, when I look at people through Jesus' eyes, then I am beginning to apply narrative concepts.

One thing I have especially been challenged about is how I speak about those in my church who seem to often be the centre of conflict or strife. It is easy to label people – to refer to 'difficult', or 'frustrating' people. And once labelled, it is easy to overlook the unique outcomes of those labels. Yes, someone may be difficult to deal with, but there are always exceptions – even when they are hard to find.

I consciously choose to speak about people (as I have learnt through discussing practice examples in class) as though they were present. I choose to look for the exceptions to the problem stories that we are so often confronted with. There will be times when a judgment call needs to be made, when those in positions of responsibility need to be disciplined or challenged, when sin needs to be confronted. But even these can be handled with respect and by being alert to unique outcomes.

In looking back, particularly at painful experiences, my husband and I have tried to discover unique outcomes to these problem situations, and to find the preferred story underlying our experiences. We have 'practiced' these new ways of looking at people and circumstances, and have made conscious decisions about how we will speak about others.

In the past as we have spoken to other people about these painful experiences we have not always been respectful in the language we have used or the attitude we have demonstrated. We now consciously choose to speak out, to proclaim, the preferred story and to be committed to seeking unique outcomes in the stories of people we encounter, and in the ongoing story that God is creating for us.

John and Jo-anne's reflections are examples of the process of engaging with Narrative ideas and practices and their impact at multiple levels of thinking and being. Not only have their practice changed but their ways of thinking about pastoral care, preaching, church life – and even of people and their spiritual journey, has been influenced by more respectful - more biblical ways of thinking and being.

References

King, D. (1999). An introduction to narrative Christian therapy. *Carer and Counsellor, 9, 1, pp34-39.*

Oates, W. (1974). *Pastoral counselling.* Philadelphia, PA: Westminster Press

Vitz, P. C. (1996). Narratives and counselling. *Carer and Counsellor, 6, 3, pp17-25.*

Chapter 13: Narrative and its possibilities for Emergent faith communities

Richard Cook

About the author

I have always been interested in people who blaze new trails and try new things. My years as a pastor led me into a few experiments of how we met and 'did church'. During my years in private counselling practice I met a number of people who were trying alternative ways of meeting as Christian believers. Then I came across the Emergent (or sometimes called Emerging) Church movement. This chapter offers some ways that Narrative ideas could be incorporated into this innovative way of being disciples together.

Introduction

Throughout the history of the church there have been small groups of Christians meeting to share their faith, express their worship and reach out to their world. In contrast to the systemic, institutional church, the early church, the Montanists, the Franciscans, the Waldensians, the Pietists, the Wesleyans and in our time the Chinese underground church, house churches and cell groups have all carried on this search for authentic and relational faith community.

Each of these movements were responding to the church and wider culture of their time – often reaching for a more intimate expression of faith than the larger institution offered. The church has always been evolving – most of the pattern of contemporary church life was born out of adaptations to culture in another time. As Gibbs and Bolger describe

> ...it is a pilgrim church... always in the process of becoming...It 'emerges' as it engages the complex mosaic of cultures... it is morphed in those cultures and exerts a redemptive influence on them (2005, p. 43).

In the last decade a new movement of small faith communities has become visible. As Karen Ward called it in 1999 on her website www.emergingchurch.org, the emerging or emergent church conversation as it is now interchangeably called, has developed. It has emerged out of the traditions of the Seeker service phenomenon, the GenX churches, the Youth Congregations and then the Young Leaders Network. Researchers Eddie Gibbs and Ryan Bolger, as a result of a four year study identified the emergent church as having one overriding hallmark – it is seeking to address what is perceived as the "philosophical disconnection [of the contemporary church] with the wider culture" (2005, p. 32).

In his study of emerging churches, Regent University's Dan Carson agrees (2005). He sees emerging churches as reading the postmodern culture, acknowledging how it shapes the understandings of life and faith in our time and responding to the changes of this era with new forms of community, worship and mission. This movement is widespread but as Carson (2005) says, it is amorphous and its boundaries are not easy to define. Many groups have no public presence or websites, preferring to just get on with living a life of community and faith.

Pioneer Karen Ward sees this movement as still in its infant stage, still coming and still emerging, but it has already been named "the emerging reformation" (Carson, 2005, p. 42). There are a number of characteristics these researchers have identified that make it reformatory as a movement.

The common characteristics of the Emergent project

Gibbs and Bolger's research involved interviewing and analysing documents from 50 case studies of emergent faith communities in the UK and USA. These groups are small (usually less than 30 people) and when they meet, do so in homes, cafes, clubs, bars and other community settings. These groups are summarised in Mark Scandrette's words as having a focus on

> Kingdom theology, the inner life, friendship/
> community, justice, earth keeping, inclusivity and
> inspirational leadership. Additionally, the arts are in a
> renaissance, as are the classical spiritual disciplines.
> Overall it is a quest for a holistic spirituality (Gibbs &
> Bolger, 2005, p.42).

Commonly, emergent churches seek to overcome dualisms and binaries of modernism such as the sacred and secular split, the body and the mind/spirit dichotomy, distinctions between male and female roles, clergy and laity, leader and follower, evangelism and social action, individual and community, outsider and insider, material and immaterial, belief and action, theology and ethics, public and private. They also seek to eradicate idea of church being a place, a meeting or a time – preferring to see church as a way of life, a rhythm, a community and a movement (Gibbs & Bolger, 2005, p236).

Gibbs and Bolger's analysis of their data from interview and group documents yielded nine common intentions and practices among emergent church communities (2005):

1)   There is commonly a desire to identify with the life of Jesus, to embrace the mission of creating an alternative and counter-cultural, socially transformative community, anti-institutional and anti-individualised, focussed on the Kingdom of God and based around servanthood and forgiveness.

2)   There is a commitment to transform the secular realm, discerning those parts of church life rooted in modernism, overcoming the focus on what is popular and attractive, linear thinking about faith as propositions, dualisms and creating "a whole-life spirituality in all realms of society" (p88).

3)   Centred on Jesus and the Kingdom come, there is a rejection of consumerism, preferring to live highly communal lives of connectedness and participation.

4)   Rejecting exclusion and conformity, there is the welcoming of the stranger, of difference and of diversity including that of faith, culture and tradition and instead of evangelistic strategies, a desire for genuine interaction with others outside of the community itself.

5)   Sceptical of programmes, the filling of church positions, meeting church budgets and building programmes, there is commonly an involvement in social care and change activity that engages with the whole person, serving with generosity and welcoming any who wish to join them.

6)   "Participating as producers" means moving away from orchestrated formulaic services with people as audience to an organic expression of the participants' own journey and experience of life and faith in open and contributory gatherings where people "bring their world to worship" (p.172).

7)   The imagination and creativity features in emergent communities where people are able to create as created beings, bringing materials, artefacts and expressions from their own world and in their own way as contributions to worship.

8)   Leading as a body was another theme meaning the creation of non-hierarchical and non-controlling communities marked by servanthood, consensus, collaboration, team spirit and facilitation in a permission-giving, empowering environment.

9)   Rejecting formulae, there is the integration of mind and body, ancient and modern in worship experience with an exploration of spiritual disciplines and a mutual participation in spiritual activities.

Carson (2005) in his review of emergent church literature also identifies a number of noticeable characteristics. He found a consistent protest and thereby a rejection of leadership where the pastor is a kind of CEO who puts clear lines of authority in place and is prone to linear and analytical stances in (usually his) presentation. Instead he noted a search for authentic expression of individuals' journey of faith and an exercising of tolerance of difference and diversity. This is similar to Gibbs and Bolger's (2005) findings that a leadership style is preferred that creates or facilitates an environment in which expression and journey can be explored.

Mike Yaconelli (2003) furthers this with a rejection of a desire for efficiency in church life, of pretending, of a life centred on doing and on faith as a set of propositions. A preferred emergent expression has unedited services where people read what they what, interrupt sermons with questions, offer alternative views and illustrations and share stories of what is going on inside and where as one of his inspirations, Henri Nouwen, described it, "God's fingerprints on our lives" can be shared (Nouwen, 1993, p20). Similarly, Todd Hunter (Carson, 2005) rejects church life focussing on programmes in favour of personalised pastoral care, theological reflection, contemplative prayer and intergenerational community.

Another area of protest seen in emergent churches is resistance to modernist views of epistemology – how we know or think we know things. Here again there is a move away from linear thinking, dichotomies, absolutism, certainty, rationalism and the intellectual from a critique of those things as tending to produce arrogance, a claim of right-ness and a desire to control. Instead there is a desire to acknowledge that what we know is culturally shaped, a move towards relational encounter, dialogue, emotion, life narratives, a study of Biblical narratives, mission as relationship, care for the poor and an embracing of paradox (Carson, 2005).

Also protested is the mega-church, traditional evangelicalism and seeker-sensitive church expression. Instead there is an acceptance of pluralism, of diversity, of experiential Christianity, of the mystical, of narrative, of the fluid, the global, the communal and of active participation (Kimball, 2003).

In his writings Carson notes a rejection of evangelicalism as a sales pitch, a conquest, of language of warfare, of ultimatums, threats, proof, argument, entertainment, show and monologue. As an example, Brian McLaren (2002), a prominent writer in the Emergent movement speaks for evangelism instead as disciple-making, conversation, friendship, influence, companionship, challenge, opportunity and a sense of a dance.

The potential of Narrative ideas and practices to nurture Emergent churches

Narrative ideas and practices can be utilised to nurture these distinctives in Emergent church communities. 1 Corinthians 14:26 calls on the body of believers to each bring contributions such as songs, words and worship when they come together. This will be illustrated in practice in these outlines of four emergent gatherings based on actual events over a number of years in such a group. Each of the two themes is first identified and is followed by a number of activity sections to explore that theme over a two-week period.

For each outline, the Starter is a warm up to focus attention on the theme. The Exploration section is to use Narrative processes to deconstruct dominant ideas and practices in the experiences of the group members and to map out the effects of these in their lives. The Links to scripture themes section brings the group to focus on broad themes in the Hebrew and Christian scriptures that relate to the topic being considered and also to identify questions for research and exegesis between that week and the next. This is in order to deconstruct the text to find the likely or possible original meaning of the author and their readers.

The Links to life section is for small groupings to get together for dialogue on some focus questions around the theme and their connection with it. This leads to the Bubbling questions part where questions people are sitting with in the group can be written up on a large poster ready for the contemplation time and also to take away for reflection during the week. During the Contemplation time, group members silently consider what questions, connections, desires and intentions are arising for them as a result of the exploration. This can be enhanced by a variety of media and opportunities to represent thoughts and feelings visually and leads well into the Reflection time where anyone can share with the group the impact of the time on them personally as well as offer songs, readings and contributions of worship to God. The gathering concludes with Planning for next time where the group takes responsibility for things they would like to contribute or suggest to do in sharing or worship at the next gathering. The plans for four of these gatherings are given below:

Week 1: Theme: Ideas and Practices of Christian Leadership.

STARTER: a quote from any text on leadership to focus attention on the theme. For example: "If we are to claim Jesus as our God, we would have to conclude that our God does not want to be served by us, he wants to serve us; he does not want to be given the highest possible rank and status in our society, he wants to take the lowest place (Nolan, p. 137-138)

EXPLORATION:
- Use Narrative ideas to explore the dominant practices of Christian leadership that people have experienced and to map out the effects of those.
- Identify the ideas behind those practices, who benefits from them and the power relations that are invoked by the ideas.
- Map the history of people's experience of these ideas and practices of leadership to show how they have been put into certain power positions and the effects of these.
- Map out what happens to people's sense of agency, how surveillance, norms and the social gaze can set up a binary of acceptance and rejection, approval and disapproval, success and failure.

LINKS TO SCRIPTURE THEMES:
- Use the focus question, "What themes in scripture relate to this topic?" to identify key ideas about leadership from biblical stories.
- Pose the follow-up question, "If you wanted to understand what these stories or teachings meant for the speaker and his listeners, what questions would you need to answer?"

- Record responses on a chart and invite people to take one or more questions away with them to search out some insights before the next gathering.

LINKS TO LIFE:
- Hold a Narrative-style interview
- Ask the volunteer about their personal experience of being a leader with a non-judgemental focus on actual practices of leading. Explore the dominant discourses inspiring these practices and the kind of professional or role identity conclusions that they fostered identified.
- Map the effects of these ideas on the person's view of those being led and the task of leadership – in other words, how these ideas constructed their identity and outworking of the relationship of leader to follower.
- In small groups hold an Outsider Witness process (White, 2007). Use four questions to guide their reflection on the interview they have just witnessed:
  1. What particular expressions stood out for you?
  2. What images/pictures are sparked by this?
  3. What do you resonate with? What does this indicate you really value?
  4. Where has this taken you?

- Create a human sculpture to represent one or more of the key ideas discussed and the helpful or hindering effects of these ideas on others.
- Groups then feed their sharing back to the whole group and show the sculpture they have created.

BUBBLING QUESTIONS: add to the chart those questions that have come to mind for people.

CONTEMPLATION: Here silence is valuable in order for people to write about, think about or draw their responses, connections, desires or intentions and then to speak them out to God or lay their words or drawings in the shared space in the centre of the group and light a candle of dedication to the Lord. Lament can also be invited here – words of sorrow at leadership exercised by them over others in harmful ways or exercised over them in ways that limited or damaged them.

REFLECTION: invite people to share something from their contemplation – something of how the time together has impacted them and how it has been for them.

PLANNING FOR NEXT TIME: conclude by sharing any ideas for how this theme might be explored or what people would like to contribute or do next time. Invite group members to take questions away to research or to come with particular kinds of contributions. End with a shared meal that people have contributed to. Invite friends or family or others they have met to join.

Week 2: Theme: Ideas and Practices of Christian Leadership

STARTER: A short piece of dialogue in a written script – for example, three 30 second interchanges between a leader and a follower that positions the leader first as CEO to employee, then parent to child and then as facilitator to co-member.

RECAP: go over the key points and questions from the previous week in order to orient anyone who wasn't there so they are not excluded from the interaction that follows.

LINKS TO LIFE: Use Michael White's ideas around what is absent from but implicit within people's concerns and complaints as the basis of the time. In a one-to-one interview or in small groups consider questions such as, "What most concerns you about practices of Christian leadership that have impacted you negatively? So, you're not saying it, but what does that concern implicitly indicate that you value in human relationship? What does the concern show is important to you? What is the history of that value in your life? Where did you learn it? Who modelled it? What are its effects? What practices does it produce?"

LINKS TO SCRIPTURE THEMES: invite people to share their findings from their exegesis or research into the questions they took away the previous week. Ask, "What did Jesus mean in his phrase, 'don't lord it over'? What did you find out about how different Jesus' call to his disciples not to lord it over was from the culture of the day? When Samuel told the people they only needed God as their King, what were the ideas behind that? What practices did the demand for a king lead to? How would it have been different if they had taken up Samuel's ideas?"

LINKS TO POSSIBILITIES: Narrative can help guide an exploration of threads of subordinate storylines – that is, almost invisible, almost unheard ideas that inspire different sorts of practices of Christian leadership. Use questions such as: "Can you tell a story of a leadership situation that was really empowering? What was it about that situation that made it energising? What ideas do you guess were inspiring that way of being? What positions were created by those ideas? What were the effects on you and others? Were these effects okay for you and others? Why is that? In terms of what you value, what are they in harmony with? What expressions do you give to this value in your life now? Why do you hold on to these values given the realities of life as you find it?"

Have groups create a statue using their bodies or create something visual that represents one inspiring idea that has emerged in their discussion and take a digital photo of their representation.

CONTEMPLATION: show the digital photo representations and explain if necessary. In a time of silence, invite people to draw or diagram or write in a personal visual diary something that has become clear for them about what they value and what they want to reproduce in their own life and relationships.

REFLECTING share these representations as well as any other contributions people have brought. Conclude with a period of prayer, both silent and aloud in whatever way people desire.

PLANNING FOR NEXT TIME: the person facilitating the next gathering invites any particular contributions on the next theme before sharing a meal together.

Week 3: Society, Christian Culture and Kingdom Culture.

STARTER: The clip from the movie "The Matrix" where Morpheus is explaining what the Matrix is to the character Neo saying that the world we think we know is just a fabrication that keeps us from seeing Reality as it is.

EXPLORATION: The whole group discusses the ways in which culture is passed on to children. Together develop a filmstrip with each frame depicting ideas and practices that children are conformed by from an early age – both helpfully and in ways that develop unhelpful conclusions about identity and behaviour in the social world. Map some of the expectations that are passed on in Christian culture along with how they are communicated and enforced in various Christian communities. In pairs, produce posters showing one unhelpful Christian cultural expectation they have experienced, together with the effects of that expectation.

LINKS TO SCRIPTURE THEMES: Identify broad themes from scripture relating to the power of social shaping, the call to disciples to create alternative culture and what that culture can look like. Write up on a chart questions that people need answering to better understand the original meaning of these scriptural themes and invite people to take them away to research.

LINKS TO LIFE: Use White's ideas around 'Migration of identity' (2007). The focus here is on how people have migrated from conformity to the patterns of the social world (Romans 12:2) to something inspired by God and His Word. The following questions are for a whole group dialogue:
1.   What social or Christian cultural ideas and practices have you been aware of and in some way separating from? Is there an image or picture for this movement?

2.   How have you prepared for these separations? What inspired them?

3.   What has been involved in the transition process?

4.   What sustains the separation through this transition?

5.   What are your hopes for the end-point of this migration process?

BUBBLING QUESTIONS: identify these and record on the chart and leave them with people for consideration.

CONTEMPLATION: Spread a number of photos on the floor and have people choose one or two that appeal to them as a result of the discussion. They may not know why they are drawn to a photo at first. Then in silence consider the connections people are making and then speak out or write out a communication to God on their migration from unhelpful social and Christian cultural ways.

REFLECTION: share these connections and each person's sense of migration.

PLANNING FOR NEXT TIME: Give questions for people to take away and invite any contributions for next time.

Week 4: Theme: Society, Christian Culture and Kingdom Culture.

STARTER: Play the end of "The Matrix" movie where Neo has broken free of the Matrix and is able to function in the constructed world without it affecting him. This sets the scene for a consideration of how a focus on the Kingdom of God can and has enabled people to step outside social conformity in some ways that are important to them.

RECAP: summarise the exploration from the previous week for those who weren't there.

LINKS TO LIFE: invite any contributions of symbols, objects, pictures, songs or music that people have brought along and invite each person to share the significance of that item to them. In small groups use a resource like the Innovative Resources "Strengths Cards" or other inspirational cards to initiate conversations around questions such as, "What social or Christian expectations have you become aware of since we spoke last time – or in the last while? What power do these expectations have on you? How do they get that power? What effects do they have? Are these effects okay for you? Why or why not? What does your objection to these expectations mean that you value instead? What is important to you that these ideas impinge upon?"

LINKS TO SCRIPTURE THEMES: Share findings from the questions people took away last time to research. Discuss, "What story are these Biblical narratives telling about the culture of the Kingdom of God? What do they say to us today about behavioural change, inner transformation, a journey of faith or submission to the community? What do you find inspiring about these Biblical ideas? What might they inspire in us as a community?"

LINKS TO POSSIBILITIES: Bring to light the subordinate storylines about Kingdom culture by addressing, in small groups, the following questions, "What's story you could tell of experiencing what you would call Kingdom culture? What were the effects of this way of being together with others? Were these effects okay for you? Why is that? What values were these effects in harmony with? What does this tell you about what's important for you? What inspired these values? Where or how did you develop them? How do you give expression to these values in small ways in your life now? How do we give expression to these values in our life together and how could we grow that expression?"

Ask the group to produce a collage using creative materials to represent one of these values in some symbolic or abstract way.

CONTEMPLATION: Share the collage with the wider group. Play any music that people have brought and invite people to write or draw in a visual diary about the impact of this exploration.

REFLECTION: Share these insights and join together in any songs of worship or declaration people have brought that reflect something of their understanding of the Kingdom of God and life lived with the Kingdom in focus.

PLANNING FOR NEXT TIME: Announce the upcoming theme and invite contributions for next time before sharing the meal together.

Conclusion

These outlines show how Narrative interactions can enhance the life of emergent faith communities. They give a range of possibilities for using deconstruction of dominant social ideas and practices and the re-storying of life guided by scripture. They maintain the Narrative stance of curiosity rather than judgement and of description rather than prescription. They offer inclusivity where people's own journey, values and differences of perspective and choice can be welcomed. While needing one or more facilitators, they promote a shared leadership with attention to dynamics of power and positioning and make space for creativity. They have the potential to lead to social involvement in just and transformative ways and offer Narrative practices to nurture the emergent expression of church community with, its participatory worship and its joining with the mission of Jesus Christ on earth.

References

Carson, D. (2005). *Becoming conversant with the emerging church: Understanding a movement and its implications.* Grand Rapids: Zondervan

Gibbs, E., & Bolger, R. (2005). *Emerging churches: Creating Christian community in postmodern cultures.* Grand Rapids: Baker Academic.

Kimball, D. (2003). *The emerging church: Vintage Christianity for new generations.* Grand Rapids: Zondervan.

McLaren, B. (2002). *More ready than you realize: Evangelism as dance in the postmodern matrix*. Grand Rapids: Zondervan.

Nouwen, H. (1993). *In the name of Jesus*. New York: Crossroad.

Nolan, A. (1976). *Jesus before Christianity: The gospel of liberation*. London: Darton, Longman & Todd.

Yaconelli, M. (2003). *Stories of emergence: Moving from absolute to authentic*. Grand Rapids: Zondervan.

Postscript

The voices represented in this text have articulated possibilities for a fruitful relationship between Christian faith and Narrative ideas as well as practical possibilities for integrating this approach into the helping professions.

Our hope is that this is part of the ongoing conversation of ways to engage therapeutically with others in our various spheres of transformational work.

Richard Cook and Irene Alexander